Lives in Cricket: No 19

Frank Sugg

A Man For All Seasons

Martin Howe

First published in Great Britain by
Association of Cricket Statisticians and Historians
Cardiff CF11 9XR

British Library Cataloguing-in-Publication Data.
A catalogue record for this book is available from the British Library.

ISBN: 978 1 908165 05 3
Typeset by Limlow Books

Contents

Frank Sugg posing in his role as a smiter.

Introduction

When the editor of this series asked me if I would write a biography of Frank Sugg I was at first reluctant to do so. All my publications to that date had been on Yorkshire cricket and Yorkshire cricketers and I thought that I should stick to that territory. However, although Frank Sugg made his cricket reputation with Lancashire, he did spend his formative and early sporting years in Sheffield and his first appearance in first-class cricket was for Yorkshire. He also played football for Sheffield Wednesday, the team I have supported since a boy. I also recalled that there was a Sugg sports business, indeed that my father had bought my first cricket bat, a Sugg bat, at the Sugg shop in Sheffield soon after the war. So there were Yorkshire and personal connections. My interest was aroused and I agreed to the request.

I soon found that there was more to Frank Sugg's life than I had realised and furthermore that the facts on certain aspects of his life were difficult to establish with any certainty. For a long time I felt that, unless I could resolve these uncertainties, there was little point in trying to write about his life. Frank Sugg's cricket career is well enough documented after all. It is a man's life outside cricket that adds to the interest of the books in the *Lives in Cricket* series. In the end, however, I concluded that, even if I had to leave some gaps, the story of Frank Sugg's life and career is one that is interesting enough to be included in the series.

I hope the reader of the book will agree.

Redbourn, Hertfordshire
April 2011

Chapter One
Not Merely a Smiter

Frank Sugg was one of the most colourful cricketers in late Victorian England. Over six feet tall and powerfully built, with a good eye and a long reach, he was a forward player renowned for his big hitting and fast scoring. 'I have cultivated hitting,' he said,[1] and he applied himself, right-handed, to the task with relish. As with Ian Botham and Andrew Flintoff in recent times, there was a buzz of anticipation among the crowd at any ground whenever he strode out to bat. It was not just the big hitting that appealed to spectators, it was also Sugg's evident enjoyment in batting, whatever the match situation.

Frank Sugg made his name in the thirteen seasons from 1887 until 1899 during which he played for Lancashire. But he was not born in the county. His birthplace was Ilkeston on the other side of the country. Sugg was one of several players who had started their careers with other counties whom Lancashire imported in the 1880s during an effort to bolster a faltering side, particularly to strengthen its batting. By the time he retired from first-class cricket at the end of the 1899 season, Frank had scored 9,620 runs for Lancashire with 15 centuries, more than any other Lancashire batsman at that time. In all first-class cricket he scored 11,859 runs and made 16 centuries. This record may not be quite good enough to put him in the first rank of cricketers in the years that began cricket's Golden Age, but they were solid achievements by any standard. It should be added that Sugg was also an outstanding fielder with a safe pair of hands and a strong throw.

Frank's reputation was not based just on his prowess at cricket. He excelled at several other sports and he ran a successful business based in Liverpool, then a prosperous port and industrial city. He played football for a number of leading northern clubs in the years before the Football League was established in 1888 and he was still young and fit enough to play a few games for Everton after that

1 Interviewed on the eve of his benefit match in June 1897: newspaper cutting provided by Malcolm Lorimer, newspaper not identified.

seminal date. He was a good golfer; he excelled at athletic events that drew on his strength and stamina; and he was a long-distance swimmer of considerable standing. While it was the physical demands of these sports that appealed to him, he also enjoyed the more leisurely pursuits of bowls, billiards and rifle shooting and was good enough to carry off the prizes in many local competitions.

Frank Sugg was indeed an allround sportsman *par excellence*, taking part in competitive activity throughout the year. He looked after himself, as the modern phrase has it, by following a regime of regular exercise throughout his sporting career and beyond. It is notable that, in cricket, where we have comprehensive information, Sugg hardly ever missed a match through injury.

Intelligent and ambitious, from an early age Frank was keen to do well in life. He wanted the good things that money could buy. Very much a realist, Frank knew that, however successful he was, the financial rewards for a professional sportsman would be modest and his future never secure. In 1890 an established player with Lancashire - who were better employers than many counties - could expect to earn £3 a week, plus match pay and talent money, during the season.[2] A sportsman's career could be cut short at any time by injury, loss of form or the whims of a club's committee, leaving him without any means of support. At an early age Frank had shown a talent for business and in 1888 he made his first serious venture into the commercial world by establishing, with his brother Walter, also an allround sportsman and professional cricketer, in his case with Derbyshire, a sports outfitters' business with its first shop in Liverpool. The business grew in the years up to the Great War when, as Frank Sugg Ltd, it was one of the leading businesses of its type, manufacturing and retailing a wide range of clothes and equipment for different sports and outdoor pastimes. In the harsher economic climate that prevailed after the War, the company, like many similar businesses, ran into difficulties, and its eventual collapse, combined with the failure of a number of more speculative ventures, cost Frank much grief and money. As will be explained in a later chapter an offshoot of Frank Sugg Ltd, HHB Sugg Ltd, run initially by Walter Sugg's son, continued to trade until 2001.

---

2 A.W.Ledbrooke, *Lancashire County Cricket, 1864-1953*, Phoenix House, 1954, p 272.

Frank Sugg was well liked by his fellow cricketers and counted many of the leading players of his day among his friends. Middle class himself, he got on well with people from all walks of life at a time when hierarchies of class were built into society and dominated social relationships. Ranjitsinhji was a particular friend and Sugg regularly visited the Prince's house, often greeted with a gift of some sort such as the ivory-carved napkin ring still in the family's possession. One newspaper described him, on his retirement, as 'one of nature's gentlemen, apart from being one by birth and education.'[3] The convivial atmosphere of the various sports and social clubs to which he belonged suited Frank perfectly. Aside from the enjoyment of others' company, he appreciated the social and commercial benefits of what we now call networking and he carefully cultivated the contacts he made from his many sporting interests and in his business life.

A Wills cigarette card of 1896 with Frank in promenade garb. Sugg's annuals later recommended young men not to smoke.

Never content to be a bystander, Frank loved conversation and was always ready to give his opinions on any subject. Favoured with a good memory, he described himself as 'a born storyteller' with a mind that was 'a treasure house of tales.'[4] To one contemporary, he was 'one of the best storytellers that cricket has ever known.'[5] Frank liked to be the centre of attention. Contemporaries recall him strolling about town or around the ground in striped blazer and a favourite straw boater, a debonair figure indeed, happy to chat with any acquaintance he encountered. He cultivated a reputation for being 'a bit of a lad' and a show-off. A favourite stunt was to ride his bicycle at full tilt along and off the end of a pier on the Isle of Man (where he took his family for summer holidays), remove his outer clothing while under water and resurface clad in his woollen swimming costume. At social functions he might startle the guests by leaping across a

3 A scrapbook of newspaper cuttings kept by Frank Sugg is in the possession of Lorna Brown, his granddaughter. Unfortunately few of the cuttings are dated or the newspaper identified. Hereafter this source is cited as Lorna Brown cuttings.

4 *Sporting Chronicle,* 25 July 1916.

5 J.A.H.Catton, *Wickets and Goals*, Chapman and Hall, 1926, p 39.

conveniently placed occasional table. His high spirits could take bizarre forms. According to family legend, Frank perched a pet animal on his shoulder for a formal photograph taken at his wedding. To give zest to another wedding celebration, Frank apparently arranged for a works brass band to greet a daughter and her husband when they emerged from church. There seems little doubt that Frank would have been something of a dressing-room prankster.

Fading glories.
Photograph taken at his wedding celebration in 1889, with perhaps a pet animal making an appearance on his left shoulder.

Other players have scored more runs for Lancashire and have received more recognition at the Test match level than Frank Sugg. His reputation rests not on the statistics of his long career, but on the manner in which he made his runs. As one newspaper report put it on the eve of his benefit match in 1897:

> Short or long as his stay at the wickets may be, he never fails to give joy to the spectators. There is something - we must not use the word offensively - rollicking in his style. He must get at the ball, and if possible send it to the far boundary. We have heard it said that 'one hour of Sugg is worth ten hours of a stonewaller' and for ourselves we regard the expression as

> literally true. Not that Sugg is a mere smiter or slogger and nothing more. We have seen him play what (for him) is a very careful game indeed. He could not have made his scores without defensive powers. But when other men beat about the bush, he, if the occasion at all warrants it, goes into the open. He is not so much a slogger as a hard hitter.[6]

When Frank Sugg's other achievements are added to the story of his cricket career, he emerges as one of the more interesting men to have played for Lancashire in the county club's long history. We shall also find that the story of his life is not as straightforward as might have been supposed.

6 *Manchester Guardian*, 7 June 1897.

Chapter Two

Family Background and Early Days

Sugg is not a very common surname - it is Saxon in origin and apparently meant either a sow or a sparrow, probably originally a nickname - and the main concentration of Suggs in the first half of the nineteenth century was to be found in the western counties.[7] While agriculture was the main source of employment, Frank Sugg's grandfather, William Nathaniel Sugg, was an iron founder. Frank's father, Hubert Henri Sugg, was born in Exeter in 1833. Hubert was actually christened Hubert Honary, Honary being an old family name of the Suggs (suggesting perhaps that the family was one of some standing), but Hubert's birth certificate gave his second name as Henri and this is the name by which he was generally known thereafter. The 1851 census lists Hubert as an accountant and it may well be that as a young man he was working in such a capacity in his father's business.

There was a considerable migration of population in the nineteenth century from the agricultural areas of the country to London and to the industrial towns of the Midlands and the North. At some stage Hubert joined the tide and moved from Devon to Sheffield. We do not know precisely when or why he went to Sheffield, though his connections with the iron trade might have been a factor. Once settled in Sheffield, Hubert qualified as a solicitor, in which profession he was to earn a good living.

In Sheffield Hubert met Ellen Howe, two years his senior, whose father was also a solicitor. The couple were married in March 1858. Their first child, Emily, was born in Sheffield in 1860. Shortly after this event, Hubert moved his family to Ilkeston, a small town in Derbyshire close to the border with Nottinghamshire. The reasons for this move are not known. Interviewed in 1896, Frank said 'it was only during a chance visit of my parents to Derbyshire that I

---

7 This information from Christopher Sugg, *Origins and Migrations of Sugg Families in England,* 2003. There is no mention of Frank Sugg and his family in this booklet but Christopher helped me with information on Frank Sugg's family.

was born there.'[8] However, chance visit or not, Hubert and Ellen chose to live in Ilkeston for a number of years. In the middle of the nineteenth century Ilkeston was changing from a market town serving a largely agricultural area into an expanding industrial centre based on local deposits of coal, iron ore, limestone and clay. Hubert perhaps saw new opportunities in the town to make use of his legal knowledge. Whatever the reasons for the move to Ilkeston, soon after, on 21 May 1860, the Suggs' first son, Walter, was born. Then, on 11 January 1862, the Suggs had their second son, Frank Howe, his second name the maiden name of his mother.

Cricket was flourishing in this part of the Midlands at the time of the birth of the Sugg boys. The Ilkeston Cricket Club was founded as early as 1824 and it became one of the leading clubs in the area. Its standing was such that in 1851 and 1852, George Parr's All-England Eleven met twenty-two of Ilkeston on the Ilkeston Recreation Ground, the visitors winning easily on each occasion.[9] According to Frank, his father was 'a fair player' who sometimes 'assisted' the Ilkeston club although we are not told in what capacity.[10] The Suggs' house bordered the field of the local cricket club. The family would watch the cricket from their garden on a sunny day, the boys scurrying to retrieve any balls that were hit over the garden wall. It was at Ilkeston and at an early age that Walter and Frank first encountered the game of cricket.

However, the Suggs did not reside in Ilkeston for very long. When Frank was aged about four, Hubert moved the family back to Sheffield.[11] Consequently, although Frank was born in Derbyshire, he was to spend his formative years, and as we shall see begin his sporting career, in Sheffield in the county of Yorkshire.

A rapidly expanding town, renowned for its cutlery and tool-making trades, Sheffield was a leading centre for sport in the 1860s. As in the Ilkeston area, there was a large number of cricket

---

8 *Cricket*, 23 April 1896.

9 These are the matches with scorecards on the CricketArchive database. There may have been others. In 1925 the club moved to the Rutland County Cricket Ground, so called because it was sited on land once owned by the Duke of Rutland and the club became known as the Ilkeston Rutland Cricket Club. Derbyshire played first-class matches on the ground from 1925 until 1994.

10 *Sporting Chronicle*, 25 July 1916.

11 *Ibid.* Frank says that the move was while he was a baby whereas a profile in *Cricket* 12 July 1888 (and a number of other sources) says that the move to Sheffield was when he was four years old. Since the second of two daughters who died in infancy in Ilkeston died in 1886 and a surviving daughter, Sarah Ellen, was born in Sheffield in 1867, the move to Sheffield seems very likely to have been between these dates when Frank would have been about four years old.

clubs organised by churches, chapels or workplaces, or representative of districts of the town, outlying villages or particular trades or professions. The proliferation of clubs meant that the level of participation in the sport was very high and the clubs provided a thriving network of sporting and social contacts. The oldest cricket club in Sheffield was Hallam Cricket Club, established in 1805, and other leading clubs were Wednesday and Pitsmoor. Unfortunately the records of these local clubs have been largely lost as club officials discarded old minute books, correspondence files, scorecards and the like as not worth keeping.

Notable early Sheffield cricket grounds were at Darnall and then Hyde Park, but the need for better facilities led to the establishment of a ground at Bramall Lane in 1855 on the fringes of the town, away, in those days, from Sheffield's increasingly smoky atmosphere. After the foundation of Yorkshire County Cricket Club in 1863, Bramall Lane became the county club's headquarters and continued to be so until 1902. The Bramall Lane ground was to be a favourite of Frank Sugg throughout his career.

On their return from Ilkeston, the Suggs bought a house in Pitsmoor, a mile or so to the north of the centre of the town. Until the processes of industrialisation and urbanisation, and especially the growth of the steel and other heavy industries, gathered pace in Sheffield as the nineteenth century progressed, Pitsmoor was a village surrounded by farms, fields and woodlands with a scattering of small workshops and a few fine houses built for the better-off. Today Pitsmoor is a sprawling, unattractive inner suburb, but when the Suggs moved there it remained a pleasant place to live, still with plenty of open spaces and woods. Contributing to the growth of the area, a new road, Burngreave Road, had been opened in 1835 to replace the earlier turnpike road between Sheffield and Barnsley. Solid middle-class houses had been built along the new road and Hubert, now firmly established in his solicitor's practice in the town, bought one of these villas, called Fearn Lea and numbered 217. The house no longer exists but a number of others of the period survive, initially handsome three-storeyed properties, now a little neglected and in dingy surroundings.

The Sugg boys made good use of the open spaces around their home in Pitsmoor. According to Frank, 'As lads we were always playing cricket. We would get up during the summer at three or

Still rural?
Pitsmoor, Sheffield in 1880, a contemporary painting by a local artist, John Taylor.

(Courtesy of Sheffield City Council)

four in the morning and go and practise in the Pitsmoor Woods. There was a path running through those woods and we played on that because it made us bowl straight and hit straight. If we did not the ball would go into grass a foot high and among trees where we had to hunt for it. It was the straight and narrow path that led to success.'[12] Even so, it is hard to imagine Frank faithfully respecting the restraints imposed by the 'straight and narrow path' and never despatching the ball into the long grass! Even as a boy, he liked to deploy the long handle.

While Frank must have exaggerated the early hour of the lads' rising, there is no reason to question his recollection of their enthusiasm for cricket - or in the winter months for football. Boys engaged in makeshift games of cricket in streets and patches of land were a common sight at the time in Sheffield, as in other towns. Apparently Frank and Walter were nicknamed 'W.G.' and 'Richard Daft' by their pals, suggesting that even at this early age they stood out among their peers.

12 *Sporting Chronicle*, 25 July 1916.

Following in the footsteps of his brother, Frank began his schooling at Pitsmoor National School. Before the Education Act of 1870, elementary education was provided in voluntary church schools. Most were National Schools, founded by the National Society. The aim of the Society (established in 1811) was to make the Anglican (and national) religion the basis of national education and to that end to establish an Anglican church school in every parish in England and Wales. The Society provided funding for construction, teacher training and books and equipment. Between 1840 and 1860, nineteen National Schools like the one at Pitsmoor were either built or extended in Sheffield. Whatever the quality of the foundation the pupils received in the '3 Rs' and in the Christian religion, organised games would not have had a place in the curriculum of a national school. Indeed, in many schools like Pitsmoor, there would have been no facilities for play of any sort, organised or unorganised. For most children, it was in the streets that they played their games.

George Ulyett, born in 1851, had been a pupil at the Pitsmoor National School before the Suggs. By the time of Frank's enrolment in the school, George Ulyett was making a name for himself in the Sheffield area as a cricketer and footballer of great promise. He had made his first appearance for the Pitsmoor club in 1866 as a sixteen-year-old and his first-class debut for Yorkshire followed in 1873. A powerfully built man with a great sense of humour and love of practical jokes, Ulyett soon established himself as an outstanding allrounder, a fast if somewhat erratic bowler, an enthusiastic fielder and above all a hard-hitting batsman whose huge drives made him a great favourite with the crowds. 'Happy Jack' Ulyett made 25 appearances for England, 23 of them against Australia. He was the obvious role model for the young Frank Sugg. Frank must have dreamed of emulating Ulyett's feats in the first-class game. But he could hardly have imagined, as he struck his own straight drives in Pitsmoor Woods, that one day he would find himself in the same England team as 'Happy Jack.' Sadly, George Ulyett died suddenly in 1898 when only 47 years old. His funeral in Burngreave Cemetery, close to the Suggs' early family home, attracted a crowd of around 4,000 people.

After the local school, Frank attended Sheffield Free Grammar School. Founded in 1603, the school had led a somewhat nomadic and chequered existence over the following two hundred years, and by the early nineteenth century had fallen on hard times. With the growing demand for better education than the Royal Grammar School (as it became known) could provide, especially in more modern subjects than the classics, two new schools were established in Sheffield in the 1830s, the Anglican Collegiate School and the Wesleyan Wesley College. The Grammar School continued, but most of the boys were under 14 years of age and the level of educational attainment was not high. It was in this period that the Sugg brothers were pupils. The school's premises were in St George's Square. It was very Victorian, according to a contemporary description:

> It was a stone building which I think was in keeping with St George's Church. From St George's Square, you entered through a stone archway and there to the left was the small caretaker's house, and then the pathway went round to the porch into which the main door opened to the large main room of the school. The floor was stone flagged and was very cold in winter. A stove stood in the centre of the room, cracked and worn. We had no gas, and water was turned into an old stone trough at play-hours outside the school.[13]

Frank was an enthusiast for all sorts of games and we can be sure that he would have taken full advantage of anything that was on offer at the Grammar School, however rudimentary it may have been. There must have been some organised cricket. A newspaper reports that 'whilst at school Frank was forbidden to play [cricket] by the headmaster, the reason being that he broke too many windows.'[14] It is unlikely that this was an absolute ban. Frank tells us in an interview in 1896 that one of his schoolmasters, a Mr Hobbs, told him that he was a promising bowler and 'should be in the first flight'.[15] Presumably Mr Hobbs was not the headmaster! Ironically, bowling was to prove one of the lesser of Sugg's accomplishments in the first-class game.

Even before Frank had started at the Grammar School, he had lost his father. Hubert Sugg died in 1871 when he was only 38 years old. Hubert's death must have been a savage blow to Ellen. Hubert was a successful solicitor in the town with a practice that specialised in bankruptcy and insolvency proceedings. We do not know how the widowed Ellen supported herself and her four

13 James A.Figorski, King Edward VII School, *KES Magazine*, July 1948.
14 Lorna Brown cutting.
15 *Cricket*, 23 April 1896.

The Sugg family lived in this house in Brocco Bank Road, Sheffield in the 1870s.

children until she could look to her two sons to take over as the main breadwinners. (To add to Ellen's pain, a fifth child had died in infancy just six months before Hubert's death.) No doubt life was hard for a time. But we do know that at some point after the death of her husband, Ellen moved with her children to a house in Brocco Bank Road in the Hunters Bar district, to the west of Sheffield town centre. Hunters Bar was a more attractive suburb than the now increasingly grimy Pitsmoor. The family's new home was a substantial stone-built house, facing the entrance to Sheffield's Botanical Gardens. It was much nearer to the Grammar School than was the Burngreave Road house. This might even have been one of the reasons for the move.

There is no doubt that Hubert and Ellen Sugg wished their sons to follow their father into the legal profession. On leaving school Walter and Frank were articled to a Mr K.E.Binns, a Sheffield solicitor, situations no doubt arranged by their father. Articled clerks had to undergo several years of 'on-the-job' training and study in preparing for the professional examinations. The brothers did not find the life of an articled clerk very congenial. Sport was their main interest in life and they were already well-known performers locally in a number of sports. They were keen to play as much as possible. Eventually, the brothers' absences from the office to play cricket or football became so frequent and irritating to Mr Binns that he required them to make up their minds to devote themselves to the law or to sport: they could not have both, he declared.[16] This ultimatum must have given Frank and Walter serious cause for thought. They knew from personal and family experience that qualification as a solicitor would give them security and a good prospect of a comfortable income. On the other hand, even if they were to prove good enough to play cricket professionally, the brothers would have known that cricketers were paid very little and that a cricketer's career was short, even if not cut off by injury, loss of form or just bad luck. We

16 Obituary of Frank Sugg, *The Daily Independent*, 31 May 1933.

do not know the date of Mr Binns' ultimatum or the brothers' immediate response to it. We do know that neither of them completed their articles and sat their professional examinations. But it was as non-qualified solicitors' clerks that the brothers earned a living for some years. In the census of 1881 the occupation of Walter, then twenty years old, is given as solicitor's clerk, and of Frank, then eighteen years, as solicitor's clerk, out of employment on the day of the count. But in 1881 both were on the brink of breaking into top-level cricket. Walter had made his one appearance for Yorkshire in 1881 before reverting to play for the county of his birth, while in that year Frank, after successes in club cricket in Sheffield, was interesting the Yorkshire selectors. It was not to be long after these promising beginnings that the brothers were able to give up all thoughts of full-time employment in a lawyer's office and look to making a living from their talents in sport.

Yet the Sugg brothers did not turn their backs completely on the law. They were able to put their legal background to good use when later they set themselves up in business as sports outfitters. When the law impinged directly on its affairs, as in the matter of alleged infringements of patents or trademarks or in disputes over payments, it was usually Walter who took the lead in representing the firm. In one case where a supplier was suing for unpaid monies and Walter was appearing for the firm, the judge complimented him, 'You appear to know as much about law as about cricket.' When the judge declared in favour of the plaintiff, Walter Sugg commented: 'Thank you, your honour, I have been on the losing side before.'[17]

Frank was also litigious by nature. In 1902 he brought an action for damages for slander against a Liverpool cotton trader, a Mr C.S.Robinson. According to Frank, he had agreed to invest £1,000 and his brother Walter £500 at the trader's invitation but Mr Robinson claimed that the agreed transaction was in bales of cotton by weight, not in pounds sterling, and hence that the brothers' obligations were for larger sums. It seems a basic matter on which to have a misunderstanding though Frank admitted he knew nothing about cotton trading. When the cotton market collapsed, the defendant claimed compensation from the Suggs and they rejected the claim. Mr Robinson then pursued Frank Sugg

17 *Liverpool Mercury*, 13 October 1897.

to various public places, including Aintree Racecourse, where in a loud voice he called Frank a swindler, a rascal and a thief. Frank's first inclination, he told the court, was to 'give [Robinson] a good thrashing' but he was dissuaded from this by Walter and later brought the action for slander. The jury found for the plaintiff and Frank was awarded £50 in damages.[18]

In another case, Frank sued a firm of builders for damages when a brick, dislodged from the roof of his premises, killed a mongoose that Frank kept to control rats and other vermin. The case was heard in Liverpool County Court by his Lancashire colleague A.G.Steel KC, who was deputising for the indisposed judge. Mr Steel found for the defendant, Frank having failed to establish any negligence on the part of the builder.[19] This action does not show Frank Sugg in particularly good light but throughout his life Frank was quick to resort to, or threaten, legal action if he thought his rights were threatened or his reputation besmirched. The later and difficult years of the Sugg sports business were punctuated with legal claims and counter-claims involving Frank, some of them with his co-directors as the opposing party. But we are jumping ahead in his story.

18 Gerry Wolstenholme, Frank Sugg as Plaintiff?, *Derbyshire CCC Yearbook*, 1998, pp 69-73.

19 Lorna Brown cutting.

Chapter Three
Sporting Beginnings

Frank Sugg may have enjoyed many sports but cricket was undoubtedly his first love. If the early-morning knockabouts in Pitsmoor Woods demonstrated Frank's enthusiasm for cricket, his first venture into a more competitive form of the game was evidence of the entrepreneurial and organisational talents that were to be fully revealed in his adult life. With a number of his young friends, Frank formed the Clinton Cricket Club. As the youngsters had virtually no equipment and kit, they went from house to house begging for old clothes and rags which they then sold on to a second-hand dealer. They raised 35 shillings (£1.75), sufficient to purchase stumps, bats and balls.[20] Frank could hardly have thought, as he went the rounds, that he would one day be the proprietor of a sizeable business manufacturing and retailing sports equipment.

According to Frank, Clinton were not beaten for two years. No records of their games have been unearthed but we can guess that Frank would have been an important member of the side. Clinton were not the only junior side that Frank played for in his youth. He was also a member of the Pitsmoor Chorist Church Club which, tongue firmly in cheek, he referred to as 'one of the foremost clubs they ever had in Sheffield.' He added: 'The club was a champion amongst youngsters though it was a Bible class affair and it brought me before the public.'[21] It may seem strange to today's cricket followers that a decent cricket team could be put out by a Bible class. But in nineteenth-century England, religion played a much bigger part in the lives of the population than it does today with church or chapel-going a part of the weekly routine for the large majority of families. With the population enjoying rising standards of living and increased leisure time, religious bodies saw a need for - and advantages to them - of facilities for organised sport such as cricket. In towns and villages around the

---

20 *Sporting Chronicle*, 25 July 1916.
21 Interview in the *Athletic Journal*, 2 August 1887.

country there was an explosion in the number of cricket clubs linked to the local chapel or church. We do not know if Frank and his siblings were regular churchgoers, but Frank showed such promise as an allround cricketer with the Chorist Church club as to be rewarded with an invitation to play for Pitsmoor Cricket Club, a club which, without fear of contradiction, could claim to be one of the leading clubs in Sheffield town and which counted George Ulyett amongst its members.

League cricket and cup competitions did not emerge in the Sheffield area until the early 1890s - Pitsmoor entered the Hallamshire League and the West Riding League at that time - but the 'friendly' matches of Frank Sugg's time with Pitsmoor were competitive, indeed often fiercely fought, nonetheless. Matches between the big local clubs often drew big crowds. The standard of play was high with George Ulyett not the only player of first-class standard to turn out for a local side. Reverse-wise, local club cricket served as a nursery for the county sides.

The event which, in Frank's view, kick-started his career as a professional cricketer was his selection in 1880, when eighteen years old, for Mr W.R.Gilbert's self-styled All-England Eleven to play Twenty-Two of Matlock and District. A cricket impresario and a cousin of W.G.Grace and his brothers, Walter Raleigh Gilbert played for Gloucestershire between 1876 and 1886.[22] Frank was recommended to Gilbert by Tom Armitage, the Sheffield-born Yorkshire cricketer who had been one of James Lillywhite's party for the historic tour of Australia in 1876/77. It was a feather in Sugg's cap to be chosen for this match by a man of Gilbert's standing in the game, even if Gilbert would have been looking to include players who lived not too distant from Matlock. Frank justified his selection, and underlined his promise, by top-scoring in the match with 37 runs. 'To that innings,' Frank said, 'I owe a confidence which was of the greatest use. It carried me along for I thought that if I could get 37 in that company while others were not so fortunate, I could get runs on other occasions.'[23]

During the following two seasons, Frank continued to enhance his reputation by some high-scoring feats in club cricket. As was the practice at the time, his appearances were not limited to a single

22 W.R.Gilbert emigrated to Canada in 1886 after being involved in a scandal over a dressing-room theft.
23 *Sporting Chronicle*, 25 July 1916.

club though his cricket base, so to speak, remained the Pitsmoor club. Among other clubs for which Frank appeared (as reported in local newspapers) were Wednesday, Heeley, Mount Tabor, Cosmopolitans, Shrewsbury, and Law Students. On the strength of his connections with the legal profession, Frank also appeared for the Judicature Cricket Club in prestigious matches at Bramall Lane, as did his brother Walter. Indeed, Walter scored his first century in one of these matches. Although batting was Frank's forte, he also often kept wicket. If this seems an unlikely position for so tall a man, Frank had great agility, a good eye and a safe pair of hands. He was also fearless, an invaluable attribute when wickets were often fiery and wicketkeepers' protective equipment minimal.

It might be thought that Frank would have been an effective bowler. After all, he was strong and able to throw a cricket ball prodigious distances. In fact, as already noted, Frank had been marked as a promising bowler while still at school, but 'I used to bowl in the style which seems to be common to girls and when I tried to throw in I used precisely the same action.' Because his throwing brought him much ridicule, he determined, at the age of fourteen, to learn to throw properly. After much effort and practice, he succeeded in this quest but only at the price of losing his bowling action. Subsequently when called upon to bowl, whether in club or first-class cricket, Frank relied on slow lobs.[24] In one match, for Sheffield against Birmingham, he is credited with taking eight wickets for 14 runs, and thereafter any decent ball he delivered was called a 'Birmingham' ball.[25] Not that there were to be many of these in first-class cricket. In a first-class career extending over 17 seasons, Frank Sugg was to take only ten wickets.

In 1882 Frank was invited to play for Hull Town Cricket Club. This marked the commencement of his career as a professional cricketer. While quite a journey from his Sheffield home, Frank would have relished the chance to widen his horizons and broaden

---

24 Information from the profile of Frank Sugg in *Cricket*, 23 April 1896. Gerald Brodribb's 1997 book on lob bowlers, *The Lost Art*, published by Boundary Books, lists Sugg as a lob practitioner, but gives no further details. Lob bowlers were far from extinct in Sugg's time as a first-class player: indeed Walter Humphreys, bowling underarm, took 122 championship wickets for Sussex in the 1893 season. It might be added that as a batsman Sugg was particularly severe on lob bowlers, perhaps because he understood their wiles. He once hit Dr E.M.Grace for fourteen successive fours and Humphreys did not escape severe punishment on occasions.

25 Joseph Stoddart, *Men I have Met*, J.Heywood, 1889, p 61.

his cricket experience. The Hull club was formed in 1853 though it did not become firmly established until the late 1860s by which time it was one of the leading sides in the East Riding. Between 1875 and 1879 the club hosted four first-class games at its Argyle Street ground in one of which, in 1876, W.G.Grace had scored 126 out of a total of 159 for the South against the North. Apparently it was primarily for his wicketkeeping that Sugg was taken on, 'a position which he filled with credit,' but it was with the bat that Frank made his mark. Batting in 'a free and vigorous manner' and taking full advantage of the small ground, he averaged over 30 for Hull Town in the 1882 season.[26]

Frank's various successes registered with Yorkshire and during the 1882 season he was chosen to appear for Yorkshire Colts. He found the cricket more demanding than anything he had encountered so far. In one match at Bramall Lane, playing for the Colts against the First XI, Frank was bowled by Ted Peate for a duck, dropped a simple catch, and was bowled by Allen Hill in the second innings for another duck. Then in the First XI's second innings he dropped Louis Hall, to the annoyance of the crowd who were, as usual, displeased by Hall's slow scoring. After this chastening experience, Frank must have wondered whether he would be better advised to think more seriously of a legal career.

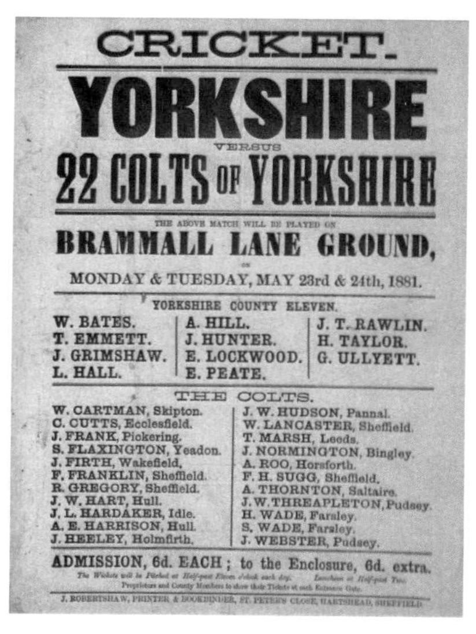

Some trial!
The full county side included six Test players. Six colts went on to play first-class cricket, some only briefly.

Nevertheless, Frank was one of a number of promising players to whom Yorkshire were looking to strengthen their team in 1883. He was one of four Yorkshire players nominated to play for the Colts of the North against Colts of the South at Lord's in the opening

26 Quotations from *Weekly Times*, 1893.

fixture of MCC's season, the first occasion on which Frank Sugg appeared in a match at cricket's headquarters. The match was a crushing victory for Colts of the North. Their southern opponents were dismissed for 43 in their first innings. The Colts of the North replied with 119. Sugg, batting at first wicket down, was clean bowled for three by John Painter of Gloucestershire. In their second innings, the southern Colts mustered 44, the Yorkshire quick bowler George Harrison taking nine for 14 off 12 overs, all nine bowled and including the hat-trick and five wickets in six balls. Despite his own modest contribution, the county showed their continuing confidence in Frank Sugg by engaging him initially for five first-class matches in the coming season, the same number as offered to Bobby Peel. Selection followed for the Yorkshire first eleven for their opening fixture against MCC at Lord's commencing on 21 May 1883. Frank could hardly have dreamed of making his first-class debut after so short an apprenticeship.

By the time that Frank Sugg was on the threshold of a career in first-class cricket, he already had a considerable reputation as a footballer with various clubs in the Sheffield area. We shall consider his career in football in a later chapter. He was also an excellent athlete, particularly in events that enabled him to use his strength to good effect such as weightlifting, putting the shot and throwing the cricket ball. He was to become something of a star turn at the latter event, his longest throw measuring 115 yards. On one occasion at Blackburn he threw a cricket ball 101 yards while standing in a bath tub to beat the 85-yard throw of his Lancashire colleague, the fast bowler Jack Crossland. Opportunities for youngsters who did not attend public schools to shine in athletics were provided by the annual athletic competitions organised by leading cricket and football clubs in Sheffield, notably Sheffield Football Club, Hallam Football and Cricket Clubs and the Wednesday Cricket Club. In the beginning, participation in these competitions was limited to club members, but by the late 1860s they had become 'open' competitions, often attracting many competitors, some from distant towns, and with admission charges for spectators. A wide variety of prizes for a wide variety of events would be on offer at these meetings. In the early days they would include 'joke' events such as wheelbarrow races or races where the competitors had to balance a bucket of water on their heads. But soon the competitions took on a more serious note. The value of prizes was increased. The conduct of the competition was more strictly organised. There were regulations on how the competitors should be dressed and the amount of flesh that could be revealed, for example. The standard of the athletics improved. The competitions of the leading clubs attracted large crowds and much local publicity and became an important source of club revenue. Betting on the results was an added attraction for many spectators. Despite the efforts of the authorities, at some venues the events featuring professional athletes were a high spot of the entertainment. As elsewhere in the country, in Victorian Sheffield the athletic competitions were an important part of the town's social scene.

Annual sports days and athletic competitions in Sheffield and other towns were organised into the 1880s. On 17 May 1883, for example, according to the *Sheffield Daily Telegraph*, 'an enormous concourse' of 20,000 people assembled at Hallam's ground at Sandygate for the football club's twentieth Annual Athletic Sports with one event (not identified) attracting as many as 77 entries. Serious athletics competitions were also held at Sheffield schools. A press cutting of 1876, when Frank Sugg was probably still a pupil, describes the great excitement and interest shown in the Grammar School sports days of the time with 4,000 people attending the ninth annual sports that year, despite bad weather.

There can be little doubt that both Frank and Walter took part in some of these competitions. There is no record of their performances but keen competition would have honed their skills in events involving running, jumping and throwing.

Cycling was also a popular pastime in Sheffield, with many cycling clubs established by the end of the century. After the enlargement of Bramall Lane in 1875, a cycle track was installed at the ground. Major cycling competitions were held there; for example in 1886 a Sheffield Cyclists' charity tournament attracted some 15,000 spectators to the ground. The facilities were also available for use by the general public in the evening for a fee of one penny. During cricket matches, a water cart would often traverse the cycle track to lay the dust thrown up by the cyclists.[27] Frank Sugg was a keen cyclist. He very probably made use of the track at Bramall Lane and he may well have participated in cycling competitions and events in the town. He continued to enjoy his cycling after his move to Lancashire. There is a nice story of him startling horses by the

27 David Hey, *A History of Sheffield*, Carnegie Publishing, 1998, p 200.

vigour with which he dismounted from his cycle outside his shop in Liverpool, having cycled in to work from his home.

Chapter Four

Playing for Yorkshire and Derbyshire

Frank Sugg played in the County Championship for 17 seasons and appeared in 239 county matches, out of his total of 305 first-class matches. He played for England a couple of times, but it was as a county cricketer that he made his reputation.

Frank's career spanned significant developments in the organisation of the Championship. In its early days, it was an informal, loosely organised affair involving a varying number of counties and fixtures, no settled way of deciding the winner of the Championship and no player qualification rules. The first steps towards a more satisfactory competition were the adoption in June 1873, on the initiative of the Surrey club, of rules on the qualification of players to represent a particular county in first-class matches. These qualification rules are important in the Frank Sugg story for in the space of five seasons he was to represent three first-class counties, Yorkshire, Derbyshire and Lancashire. This was so rare a circumstance[28] that it is worth setting out the rules in full:

> 1 No cricketer, whether amateur or professional, shall play for more than one county during the same season.
>
> 2 Every cricketer born in one county and residing in another shall be free to choose at the commencement of each season for which of those counties he will play, and shall, during that season, play for one county only.
>
> 3 A cricketer shall be qualified to play for any county in which he is residing and has resided for the previous two years, or a cricketer may elect to play for the county in which his family home is, so long as it remains open to him as an occasional residence.

---

28 In fact, Frank Sugg was the fourth player to have appeared for three different first-class counties under these provisions.

4 That, should any question arise as to the residential qualification, the same shall be left to the decision of the Marylebone Club.

The nine counties that competed in 1873 were Derbyshire, Gloucestershire, Kent, Lancashire, Middlesex, Nottinghamshire, Surrey, Sussex and Yorkshire. However, they did not all play the same number of matches and there was no agreed or consistent method of determining the winner of the Championship, by means of points, for instance. Instead, the decision was left to the judgement of the cricket press. In certain years, the accolade had been awarded to different counties by different authorities - hardly a satisfactory situation. Derbyshire dropped out of the competition in 1887, a significant event in the Frank Sugg story, as we shall see.

Further steps to regularise the County Championship were taken in meetings in December 1889 of the secretaries of the eight first-class county clubs which arranged the fixtures for the 1890 season. They determined the method by which the Championship should in future be decided, though it was to be changed as soon as 1895 - and many times thereafter. *Wisden* referred to the outcome for 1890 as 'the now officially recognised competition for the championship.' In May 1894 it was agreed that Derbyshire could re-enter the Championship in 1895 and Essex, Hampshire, Leicestershire and Warwickshire were also admitted for that season. By 1895 the structure of the competition was firmly established and, in the final step towards official recognition, MCC became responsible for awarding the Championship in that year.

Frank Sugg had resided in Yorkshire from a very young age and clearly was qualified on that count to play for Yorkshire. However, as he was born in Ilkeston, Derbyshire, his selection would appear to have infringed the Yorkshire club's own convention that only cricketers born in Yorkshire were qualified to play for the county. Exceptions had been made before, however, most notably for the Honourable Martin Bladen Hawke, later Lord Hawke, born in Willingham, Lincolnshire, whose first appearance in a long career with Yorkshire was in 1881. In fact, Frank Sugg was the fifteenth cricketer to play for Yorkshire since the county club was established in 1863 who had not been born in the county.[29] While never formally a rule of the club, the convention became so central

29 For the list, see *Yorkshire County Cricket Club Yearbook*, 1994, p 44.

to the identity of Yorkshire cricket right up to 1992, when it was finally abandoned, that some explanation of how the convention came to be ignored in Frank's case is needed. According to Frank, he owed his selection to the strong recommendation of Mr H.Stratford, a member of the county committee. At this time, Bramall Lane was the headquarters of the Yorkshire club and Sheffield members dominated the Yorkshire committee. Indeed, for the first twenty years of the club's existence, committee members were exclusively from Sheffield; with reason, the administration of the club was dubbed the 'Sheffield monopoly'. It was not until 1883 that representatives of Bradford, Dewsbury, Halifax, Huddersfield, Hull, Leeds and York were admitted to the committee and even then Sheffield members continued to be in the majority. Committee-member Stratford was one of them, and he must have known Frank personally. Presumably he was keen that a promising cricketer like Frank Sugg, who had spent all but his infancy in Sheffield and learned his cricket in the town, should not be lost to the county on the technicality that he was born outside its boundary when his father paid 'a chance visit', as Frank put it, to Ilkeston.

An intriguing footnote to this account is that Walter Sugg is another player born outside the county who played for Yorkshire, albeit a single match in 1881 and therefore before Frank's appearances. He was a competent cricketer but not in the same class as his younger brother. How Walter came to join the band of 'foreigners' who played for Yorkshire is not known. It seems most unlikely that any member of the Committee would have taken up his cause in the way Mr Stratford did for Frank. Perhaps the reason is no more complicated than that the convention was applied less rigorously in the county club's early years. It is worth adding that, with the exception of Lord Hawke, few of the 'foreigners' played more than a handful of games for Yorkshire.

Frank Sugg made his debut in a year of change for Yorkshire as in 1883 Lord Hawke (as he became in 1887) finally took over the captaincy from Tom Emmett under whom his lordship had chosen to play in the previous season when available, 'to pick up a few wrinkles' as he put it. Tom Emmett was an irrepressible cricketer. An excellent batsman and a fine left-arm quick bowler, his enjoyment of the game was there for all to see. He was a great favourite with the crowd. But Tom Emmett was not a thinking cricketer, nor was he a leader. The team included some talented cricketers, particularly among the bowlers, but Emmett was unable to weld his players into an effective cricketing force. There was a lack of organisation, focus and discipline. In present-day jargon, the total was less than the sum of the parts. As a consequence, Yorkshire's results in county cricket had disappointed. Lord Hawke was to change all that, and in due course his leadership was to make Yorkshire the dominant force in county cricket for two decades.

Although only a step along this road, 1883 was an excellent season for Yorkshire. They lost only two of 16 games in the Championship and, according to a number of authorities, including *Wisden,* were the champion county. Other authorities, however, and Yorkshire's official statistician, awarded the title to Nottinghamshire with Yorkshire in second place.[30] This demonstrates the confusion that reigned until an agreed scoring system was adopted for the 1890 season. But whichever ranking in 1883 was the more justified, Frank Sugg was not to share in the team's success.

By all accounts, Frank had the big-match temperament, but he must have been nervous as he began his first-class career for Yorkshire against MCC at Lord's on 21 May 1883 before a large crowd that would have included many of cricket's notables. The match was scheduled for two days only in order not to clash with the Epsom Derby. The MCC team was a powerful one and included such giants of the game as W.G.Grace, C.T.Studd, A.N. (Monkey) Hornby, who was to become so important a figure in Frank's career, and Lord Harris. Frank's keenness to do well can be imagined. MCC batted first and were dismissed for only 125. Sugg had the satisfaction of taking a couple of catches. In their first innings Yorkshire did no better than their hosts and were all out for 121. Tom Emmett, Yorkshire's captain in this match, had entrusted Frank Sugg with opening the Yorkshire innings with George Ulyett, his hero from his schoolboy days. Frank was out for 11, bowled by Arnold Rylott, a left-arm quick bowler who played for Leicestershire before they became a first-class county. After MCC had been put out a second time for 113, Frank had no chance to do better in Yorkshire's second innings as Emmett chose to

30 Robert Brooke reviews the various authorities' decision on which county had won the Championship between the years 1864 and 1889 in his *A History of the County Cricket Championship*, Guinness Publishing, 1991, at p 10. See also Peter Wynne-Thomas, The Early County Championship, in *The Cricket Statistician*, 32, 1980, pp 2-7, and Roy D. Wilkinson, *Yorkshire County Cricket Club First-Class Records*, 1863-1996, Limlow Books, 1997, p 11.

open with Ulyett and himself and the pair hit up the 118 required for victory in an unbroken stand. The match was all over inside the allotted two days.

Frank retained his place for Yorkshire's next match against Cambridge University at Fenner's.[31] The match was another low-scoring affair and was drawn after play on the final day was washed out by rain. In his one innings, Sugg, first wicket down this time, batted for twelve overs but scored only six in Yorkshire's first-innings total of 176. Sugg's next match for Yorkshire was against twenty-two Yorkshire Colts at Bramall Lane. He probably felt as much on trial as the youngsters in the twenty-two. While Yorkshire had the better of a drawn match, Sugg scored only five out of Yorkshire's 234 in their only innings. Frank must have been very disappointed with his first appearances for the county but Yorkshire's batting was not their strong suit and the selectors stuck with him. Sugg was included in the Yorkshire side in each of the first six matches in the 1883 championship campaign. These were largely successful for Yorkshire, but they were not to be so for Frank Sugg. Against Kent at Dewsbury, when Yorkshire won by an innings and 131 runs, Frank scored 10; against Sussex at Bramall Lane, in a closely fought match which Sussex won by three runs, Frank scored six and nine; against Middlesex at Lord's when Yorkshire won by five wickets, Sugg, scored eight not out, batting lower in the order, and nine when restored to the opening slot; against Nottinghamshire at Bramall Lane in a drawn match, Frank made four and 13 not out; in the return match with Nottinghamshire at Trent Bridge, when Frank played under the captaincy of Lord Hawke for the first time and the home side won by nine wickets, Frank made three not out and one not out; and finally, against Lancashire at Old Trafford, when Yorkshire won by eight wickets, Frank was bowled for a duck by R.G.Barlow. Throughout his career, Frank was to be vulnerable at the beginning of an innings and that weakness was very evident in these opening matches in his first-class career.

A total of 80 runs in his 12 first-class innings, 63 runs in 10 innings in the County Championship, with a top score of 13 not out, was a miserable start to Sugg's career. He did no better when later included in Yorkshire's side in two two-day matches against Leicestershire, then not a first-class county. Yorkshire regarded

31 Lord Hawke played for Cambridge University in this match.

these fixtures primarily as trials for promising young players though for Sugg it must have seemed a demotion, even if he had initially been engaged for just five matches. Again Frank failed with the bat. He scored only 14 runs in his three innings.

Some years later, Frank recalled keeping wicket for Yorkshire in one of his eight first-class matches for the county - with gloves that cost 2s 6d and pads 3s 6d.[32] Although on each occasion Yorkshire's regular keeper, Joseph Hunter, was in the side, Frank Sugg did take over the gloves in the Middlesex second innings at Lord's and then achieved a stumping off the bowling of William Bates. In another match, against Leicestershire at Grace Road, Hunter was absent and Frank may also have had the chance in that match to keep wicket, though if he did, he did not secure any victims. Whatever Frank Sugg's competence behind the stumps and the enjoyment he evidently took from the role, had he remained with Yorkshire he would have had no chance of supplanting Joseph Hunter.[33] As a very occasional wicketkeeper, his first-class record was to show just the one stumping.

In contrast to his modest performances for the Yorkshire county side, Frank was very successful in 1883 in club cricket. He turned out for various club sides and made a total of over 2,000 runs, averaging over 40 per innings. His highest score was 191 for Durham against Scarborough. Durham had engaged Walter Sugg for the season and were so keen to beat their Yorkshire rivals that they arranged, through Walter, to add Frank to their team just for the one match. His big century more than justified their initiative. A second century was his 109 not out for Eccleshill, a suburb of Bradford, against St Stephen's. His experiences would have indicated to Frank how large was the gap between club and first-class cricket. Success in the one is no guarantee of success in the other.

Eight matches is a decent run of first-class games for a newcomer to show what he is made of, and Frank Sugg failed to grasp the opportunity presented to him by the Yorkshire committee. He was not prepared to accept that he had had a fair chance, however: 'I was generally put in very late and never given a chance of going in early, even when I had played a not out innings.' This is

32 *Sporting Chronicle*, 25 July 1916.

33 When the time came for Joseph Hunter to give way, it was his brother David who took over the position in 1888, soon establishing himself as one in a line of distinguished Yorkshire wicketkeepers.

disingenuous, to put it mildly. In his 12 first-class innings, he batted at number five or higher on six occasions, four of the six in his first four matches. It was only as his poor form continued that Sugg was dropped to eight or nine in the order. He also complained that he had not been picked for any matches in August, which he described as 'a batsman's month'[34] and he was self-confident enough to make his feelings known to the powers that be at Yorkshire. But they had a lesser opinion than Frank of his abilities. He was guaranteed no more than three matches in the next season, and Frank's demand for more games, including three or four in August, was rejected. One can imagine how Mr J.B.Wostinholm, the autocratic Yorkshire secretary, would have reacted to such demands from a young man who had played only a handful of first-class games and with limited success. If he thought he could browbeat the secretary, Frank was proved wrong. Although he was selected for Yorkshire's match against Gloucestershire at the start of the 1884 season, Yorkshire clearly did not see him as a player for the long term. Indeed, Wostinholm informed Derbyshire that Frank Sugg was qualified to play for them as he had been born in the county. Derbyshire promptly invited Frank to play for the county in all their matches in 1884. Frank's response was to turn down the chance to play for Yorkshire against Gloucestershire and instead to accept Derbyshire's offer, remarking that 'I saw not the slightest hope of ever being regularly in the Yorkshire eleven' (presumably a barb at the authorities and not his assessment of his ability) and 'naturally I preferred to play for the county in which I was born.'[35] This has a hollow ring. Although Derbyshire were a first-class county at the time, they were one of the weaker counties and they were to drop out of the Championship in 1887.

But Frank had to earn a living. Match fees for occasional matches for Yorkshire were not enough for a young man to live on, let alone to make a respectable contribution to the budget of the Sugg household, shorn of its main breadwinner. Frank had witnessed the life of a professional cricketer at first hand and had no wish to abandon his chance of pursuing his own sporting career in favour of full-time employment, probably, given his background, as a clerk in some lawyer's office with long hours poring over and transcribing legal documents. The inducement for Frank to join a far less prestigious county than Yorkshire was the offer of a

34 *Cricket*, 23 April 1896.
35 *Ibid.*

salaried position as a clerk in the offices of John Smith, a Derby solicitor, with secretarial responsibilities that embraced both the cricket and the football clubs. The County Ground at Derby had hosted county matches since the club's formation in 1870 and it was also the home of Derby County Football Club. Frank reached an understanding with his employer that he could take time off to continue playing cricket and football, including matches for Derbyshire and for Derby County. As his match fees from Derbyshire were modest and he was not paid - at least officially - for his appearances for the football club, his wages for his secretarial duties were important to him. Frank was not the first man, and he most certainly was not the last, to combine playing and administrative involvement in his preferred sports. In Frank's case, however, the combination of roles was not to last very long.

In 1884, Derbyshire played only five other counties, home and away - Kent, Lancashire, Surrey, Sussex and Yorkshire, plus matches with MCC. Frank Sugg played in all those championship matches and in three other first-class matches. His first match for Derbyshire was against Lancashire at Old Trafford, commencing on 22 May 1884. Lancashire won by 42 runs, Frank scoring 73 and 26. Following this match, he appeared for an England XI against the touring Australians at the Aston Lower Grounds at Birmingham. The England XI was chosen and captained by Hugh Rotherham, a Warwickshire amateur who had lived in Australia for a number of years. The team included a number of other local amateurs and did not merit the accolade England XI, notwithstanding the inclusion of the Lancastrians R.G.Barlow, Johnny Briggs, Alec Watson, and Richard Pilling. At so early a stage in his career, Frank Sugg seems an odd selection but he was no doubt delighted by the opportunity it presented. The match was a remarkable one with the England XI suffering defeat in a single day. They were dismissed for 82 in their first innings with F.R.Spofforth taking seven for 34. Sugg was one of his victims, bowled for five. But the Englishmen came back strongly to dismiss the powerful Australian side for only 76, Barlow taking seven for 31. The already worn and bare wicket deteriorated as the day wore on and the England XI were bowled out in their second innings for a miserly 26. Spofforth had the sensational figures of seven for 3 off 8.3 four-ball overs. Sugg failed to score, falling this time to H.F.Boyle. Needing only 33 runs for victory, the Australians made heavy weather of the task, losing six wickets for 28 runs before the job was done. Only three batsmen reached double figures in the course of the whole game. Despite the excuse of a sub-standard pitch, Frank must have returned to his Derbyshire colleagues chastened by his experience of The Demon and his Australian teammates.

The rest of the season was to prove no more rewarding for his county or himself. All nine remaining county matches were lost, several by wide margins. Sugg's highest score in these matches was 61 in the second innings against Kent at Gravesend when Kent won by an innings and five runs. The match against Kent at Derby early in the season was notable in that it was the first first-class match in which Frank and Walter Sugg appeared in the same side. Also noteworthy was the match against Sussex at Hove when Sugg kept wicket for the first time for Derbyshire. Derbyshire also had a match against the touring Australians at Derby. The visitors won a one-sided encounter by an innings and 40 runs. Spofforth again was the main destroyer with returns of seven for 31 and five for 52. Frank scored 52 in the first innings, a splendid knock, but was out for a duck in the second. Derbyshire's only victory in the 1884 season was against MCC at Lord's, by seven runs in a closely fought match. Frank scored only five and nought. Arnold Rylott, the bowler who had dismissed Frank on his first-class debut for Yorkshire against MCC in 1883, had a hat-trick at the beginning of Derbyshire's second innings, with Frank and Walter two of his victims.

In his 26 innings in 13 first-class matches in 1884, Frank Sugg scored 439 runs at a disappointing average of 16.88 and with a top score of 73, achievements indistinguishable from those of many other journeyman players. He must have had second thoughts at the season's end on the wisdom of his decision to leave Yorkshire in favour of his native county. Despite the appearance for the England XI, he had made little impact on the wider cricket world outside Derbyshire. The limited fixture list of his county did mean that he had plenty of opportunities to play club cricket during the 1884 season, mainly for clubs in the Sheffield area. He made some big scores, including 213 for Sheffield against Hull Town, 114 for Wednesday against Eckington and 125 for Pitsmoor against Armitage Bridge in successive innings. Frustrated by his relative lack of success with Derbyshire, Frank no doubt relished the opportunity to chance his arm against club cricketers. He was never one to ease off in minor matches.

In the 1885 season Derbyshire again had ten fixtures in the County Championship, but with Hampshire taking the place of Sussex. Frank Sugg played in all ten matches, his only first-class appearances in the season. Derbyshire had more success than in the previous season defeating Lancashire in the match at Old Trafford early in the season and later beating Hampshire twice. Five matches were lost and two were drawn. Against Lancashire, Sugg scored 81 not out in Derbyshire's second innings, then the highest score of his first-class career. (Lancashire avenged this defeat in the return fixture with a ten-wicket victory, notable for Johnny Briggs' nine for 29 in Derbyshire's second innings.) At Southampton, Derbyshire beat Hampshire by an innings and 343 runs. The pleasure from so impressive a victory, albeit against another of the weaker first-class counties, was increased for Frank by his own contribution. Batting at five, he scored 187, including a six, a five and 17 fours, out of 427 in Derbyshire's innings, his first first-class century. In Nottinghamshire's comprehensive victory over Derbyshire at Derby by an innings and 250 runs, Arthur Shrewsbury and W.Flowers both scoring centuries for the visitors in their total of 451, Frank Sugg was called upon to deliver six overs of his 'insidious lobs'. He did not take a wicket but conceded only 14 runs, a not unreasonable outcome for so occasional a bowler.

Frank Sugg could feel more pleased with his performances in 1885 than with those of his disappointing first season for Derbyshire. In his 19 innings he scored 462 runs at an average of 27.17 with a top score of 187. The problem was the frequency with which he was dismissed for a very low score. In seven of his 17 completed innings, he was out for five runs or less. This was to be a feature of his career that he tried to dismiss as an inevitable consequence of his aggressive approach to batting. But he would undoubtedly have been more successful had he been more prepared to knuckle down and build an innings before launching into an attacking mode.

It was during the 1885 season that Frank took steps that were to undermine his relationship with the Derbyshire county club. The cause was Burnley, the centre of the Lancashire cotton-weaving industry, and at the time a thriving industrial town. As in other industrial towns in the late nineteenth century, interest in sport in Burnley, particularly cricket and football, was exploding. The Burnley Cricket Club had been formed in 1834 and was a major club in its area of Lancashire. In the mid-1880s a number of cricket leagues were beginning to be established, culminating in 1892 with the formation of the Lancashire League, arguably the premier of all cricket leagues. In 1882 the Burnley Football Club was formed and the footballers were encouraged by the cricket club to use a field at Turf Moor adjoining the cricket ground.

Walter Sugg was Burnley Cricket Club's professional and, no doubt on his recommendation, Frank was invited to play for the club during the town's Annual Fair celebrations, 10 to 13 July 1885. Against Keighley he scored 46, against Nelson 61, and against Macclesfield and District 107, Burnley winning all three matches. Frank was promptly offered attractive terms to continue playing for Burnley for the rest of the season when his county commitments allowed and also to play for the football club in the winter. Moreover, he was offered a secretarial position at the club. His absences from his office duties at Derby to play football in the winter had already led to criticism from his employer and the acceptance of Burnley's offer brought Frank's secretarial responsibilities at Derby to an end. He had also complained to the Derbyshire committee of irregularities by one of the county's officials, a complaint that was not acted upon. Frank accused the same official of refusing to hand over the money collected for Frank after his 187 against Hampshire in August 1885 and even, on occasions, to pay his match fee.[36] There is no way of establishing if these criticisms were justified, but they would not have endeared him to the committee at Derby while at the same time souring Frank's feelings towards the club, his employer.

Frank accepted Burnley's offer without hesitation and decided to live in the town, a decision that was to lead to his qualification to play for Lancashire. Frank confessed later he had 'just a little notion of this' at the time,[37] though he no doubt kept the implications of the thought to himself. He was to enjoy three successful seasons with Burnley where his big hitting and fast scoring made him a great favourite with the club's followers. According to one report, 'the glaziers' services were frequently required to repair damaged windows in Belvedere Road resulting from Sugg's hard hits.'[38]

---

36 *Ibid.*
37 *Athletic News*, 2 August 1887.
38 Burnley CC *Centenary Bazaar Handbook*, 1935, p 59.

Despite his increasing involvement with Burnley, Frank continued to play for Derbyshire in 1886, beginning with Derbyshire's match against MCC at Lord's and followed by nine championship and two other first-class matches, against the touring Australians and for the North against the South, but the seeds of trouble in Sugg's relationship with his county had already been sown. Derbyshire began well enough as MCC were beaten at Lord's by an innings and 28 runs. But MCC fielded a weak side, an indication perhaps of the mustard that Derbyshire cut at Lord's, and even then Sugg scored only nine. Far stronger opposition was provided by the touring Australians and in the event the visitors needed only two days to defeat the county at Derby by six wickets, Sugg scoring three and 23. It was after this match that Frank Sugg appeared for the North against the South at Lord's. Usually considerable prestige attended selection for this venerable fixture but on this occasion the two sides fell well short of representative standard. Indeed, no fewer than four of the players, three for the North, made their first-class debuts in the match. After W.G.Grace, Frank Sugg was one of the more experienced players on show. The North won by nine wickets inside two days. Sugg scored 26 and nought, hardly impressive batting - especially when John White, in his first big match, and J.T.Parnham put on 157 for the last wicket in the North's first innings of 305. In the County Championship, Derbyshire had a wretched season. Hampshire were replaced by Gloucestershire in Derbyshire's fixtures though only for one match, at home at Derby. The first match of the season against Lancashire at Old Trafford was drawn but all the other county matches were lost. Frank Sugg's contributions in 1886 were most disappointing, particularly after the encouraging season he had enjoyed in 1885. He scored 408 runs in 23 innings at an average of 17.73. His highest score was 62 against Yorkshire early in the season and in no other innings did he reach a half-century. This was not a level of performance that marked him out as a batsman of whom great things could be expected. As in previous seasons, there were too many occasions when he was dismissed early on for very low scores: in seven of his innings in 1886 he was dismissed for five runs or fewer.

Given the difficulties he was encountering in his off-the-field position at Derby, it is very likely that Frank Sugg's heart was not in his cricket for the county. Now 24 years old, he was an ambitious man and he must have realised his career was stagnating with a county that played few matches, whose county ground had poor facilities and a notoriously poor surface, and whose players

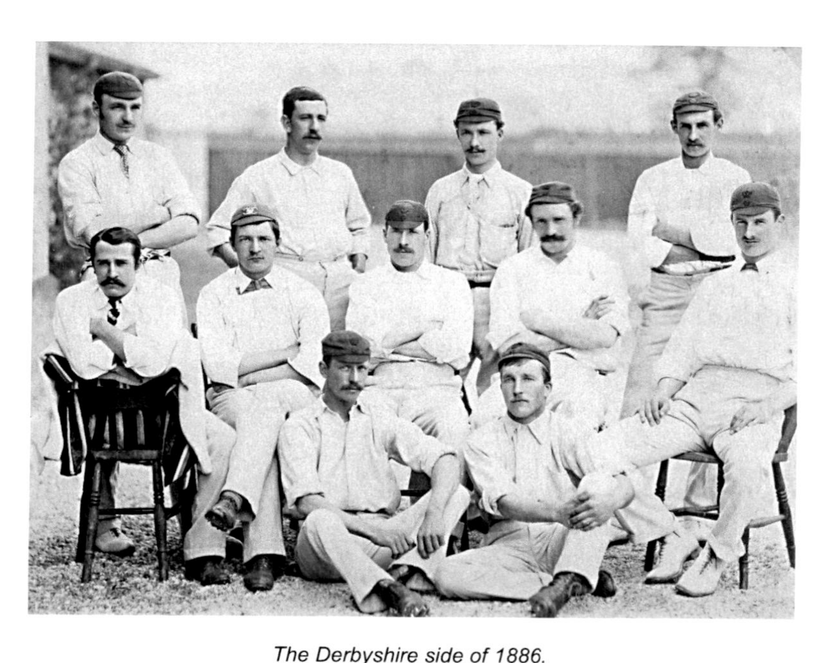

The Derbyshire side of 1886.
Standing (l to r): F.H.Sugg, W.Cropper, E.Coupe, W.Chatterton.
Seated: G.G.Walker, A.H.J.Cochrane, E.A.J.Maynard (capt), L.C.Docker, W.S.Eadie.
On the ground: J.J.Disney (wk), G.A.Davidson.
The county won one of its eleven first-class matches in this season and lost nine.

seemed to have little chance of being selected for representative matches. In his three seasons with Derbyshire, Frank Sugg had appeared in every first-class match played by the county. He would have been aware that comparisons with the leading players of the day were unfavourable but envious of the amount of first-class cricket they were able to play in the course of a season compared with Derbyshire's players. Twelve players scored 1,000 runs or more in the 1886 season; W.G.Grace, not surprisingly, was top of the list with 1,846 runs in 33 matches. And if his cricket was stagnating, then so was Frank Sugg's earning potential. Frank had become a professional cricketer not just out of love for the game but also to make some money.

After the close of the 1886 season things came to a head between Frank Sugg and Derbyshire. Frank was engaged for another season in 1887 as Burnley's cricket professional and during the preceding winter he chose to play football for Burnley rather than Derby County, a choice which naturally rankled with the county authorities in Derby. He was told that if he did not play for Derby County at football, he would not play for Derbyshire at cricket. A stubborn man, Frank stuck to his guns and did not play for Derby County at all in the 1886/87 season. According to Frank,[39] his letters to Derbyshire went unanswered. He does not say whether he was trying to get the county club to change its position and, if so, what arguments he put to them. But then, shortly before the opening match of the 1887 season, he received a letter saying he had been selected for Derbyshire for the fixture against MCC at Lord's. He wired his refusal. As well as having his fallback position with Burnley cricket club, Frank was strengthened in throwing down the gauntlet in this way by the knowledge that James Sutcliffe, later president of the Lancashire League, had recommended him to the Lancashire county committee. Although Derbyshire tried to argue otherwise, Frank understood - no doubt applying his legally trained mind to the detail of the qualification rules - that during the course of the season he would become qualified to play for Lancashire by residence. The position he took was nevertheless a risky one but, as Frank was to show throughout his life, he was never a man to shirk a risky decision.

Fortuitously for Sugg, Lancashire were keen to strengthen their playing staff by recruiting any available quality players, even those of other counties. Frank Sugg would bolster Lancashire's batting and the offer of an engagement with the county was made to take effect as soon as the two-year qualification rule was satisfied - 11 July 1887. Until then, Frank continued to play for Burnley and other club sides. When an invitation was attractive enough, he was prepared to make long journeys to play cricket. (One reflects how important to the development of cricket was the railway boom of Victorian Britain.) In a brief tour of Scotland, Sugg scored 73 and 52 for an England XI against the West of Scotland club. He then guested for West of Scotland against Bryn-y-neuadd, a Caernarvonshire side 'which included some professionals of repute', and hit 172 out of 271 and an unbeaten 42 out of 48.[40]

With his period of qualification finally out of the way, and feeling ready to renew the challenges of first-class cricket, Frank Sugg was chosen to make his debut for his new, and third, county in Lancashire's match against MCC at Lord's beginning on 21 July 1887.

---

39 *Athletic News*, 2 August 1887.
40 *The Cricketers' Yearbook*, 1888.

Chapter Five
Frank Sugg the Footballer

Although he might be better known as a cricketer, Frank Sugg was an enthusiastic and competent footballer and we will pause at this point in his story to tell of his career in his winter sport.

By the time of Frank's boyhood in Sheffield, football had become the most popular sport of the mass of the population, particularly of the working classes in the industrial towns of the North and Midlands. Sheffield emerged as a leading centre of the game and the town played a prominent part in the transformation of football from an anarchic, rough and tumble sort of game into an organised and regulated sport. A major part in this was played by Sheffield Football Club, formed in 1857 and the oldest football club in the world, and the Sheffield Football Association. It was largely the rules formulated by the Sheffield Football Association that were refined and adopted by the newly formed (English) Football Association in the mid-1860s and which brought to an end the previous chaotic situation where matches were played according to the rules of the home side. This can be said to herald the beginning of the modern game. The numerous local football clubs in Sheffield, including, amongst the more prestigious, Pitsmoor and Sheffield Wednesday (which club grew out of the Wednesday Cricket Club), as well as Sheffield Football Club, formed themselves into flourishing local leagues. A number of challenge cup competitions were also organised. Competition among the clubs in the Sheffield area was fierce, with bouts of fisticuffs between players or spectators not uncommon occurrences.

Football soon outgrew local clubs in local leagues, but until the Football League was formed in 1888, fixtures for the leading clubs consisted of English cup-ties - the FA Cup having been inaugurated in 1871 and first played for in 1872 - and friendly games of various standards, including inter-town and inter-association matches. The founder members of the Football League were Accrington Stanley, Aston Villa, Blackburn Rovers, Bolton

Wanderers, Burnley, Derby County, Everton, Notts County, Preston North End, Stoke City, West Bromwich Albion, and Wolverhampton Wanderers. Note the absence of any club from the south. The impetus for the formation of the League was the spread of professionalism in the sport though this was not finally recognised by the Football Association until 1885; before then players could play for any number of clubs so long as they were paid-up members. Of the Sheffield clubs, Sheffield Wednesday became professional in 1887 and entered the Football League when it was extended in 1891. Sheffield United, established in 1889 with their ground at Bramall Lane, also joined the Football League in 1891. Sheffield Football Club has remained an amateur club up to the present day.

This was the background to Frank Sugg's career in football. As a youth he joined in makeshift football games with his pals in the fields and lanes of Pitsmoor. They were of course much easier to set up than the cricket that they played in the summer. Frank's strength and commitment in these games marked him out from his peers and, as with his cricket, he was soon chosen for local club sides where he established himself as a brave 'no nonsense' type of player whether at centre-half, his favourite position, or at centre-forward. He could not be described as a ball player in any football sense of the term. Of course, football was a more physical and less skilful game than it is today, and that suited Frank Sugg's style of play. His ability was soon recognised by the Sheffield Football Association and he was selected for Sheffield in matches against London and Glasgow. With this recognition, Frank could expect leading football clubs of the day to be interested in making use of his services.

According to the biographical details of Frank Sugg in the cricket literature, he played for a number of major football clubs and was captain of several of them. For example, Anthony Woodhouse, the Yorkshire cricket historian, said in his *Who's Who of Yorkshire County Cricket Club*: 'He was also a first-rate footballer, captaining Sheffield Wednesday, Derby County and Burnley, as well as assisting Bolton Wanderers, Everton and West Manchester.'[41] From the other side of the Pennines, Brian Bearshaw in his *From the Stretford End: the Official History of Lancashire County Cricket Club* stated that Sugg 'had football fame with Sheffield

41 Anthony Woodhouse, *Who's Who of Yorkshire County Cricket Club*, Breeden Books, 1992, p 190.

Wednesday, Derby County, Burnley and Bolton.'[42] Other publications reported in similar fashion. The obituary of Frank in *Wisden* included the following: 'Frank Sugg was equally good at Association football and he gained fame with Sheffield Wednesday, Derby County, Burnley and Bolton Wanderers, being captain of the first three teams.'[43] There is no doubt that Frank Sugg played for these football clubs but the statements quoted may lead one to conclude that Frank was a more important player for these clubs than was actually the case.

Not surprisingly, the first club to come knocking on the Suggs' door was Sheffield Wednesday. In 1883 Frank had played for Pyebank, a local side based in the Pitsmoor district of Sheffield, against Wednesday in the final of the Wharncliffe Charity Cup. Wednesday were impressed by Sugg's performance and he subsequently appeared for them during the 1883/84 season.[44] It has not proved possible to establish how many games Frank Sugg played for Sheffield Wednesday and at what level. Documentary evidence on appearances before the formation of the Football League is hard to come by and is not always reliable. For example, there can be differences in how sources interpret 'played for' a particular football club: some might include appearances in any match for a club, others only appearances in designated major competitions. Sheffield Wednesday's own archives list all players who have appeared for the first team in a competitive match: Frank Sugg does not appear in the list. The club suggested to the writer that Sugg might have played for the reserve or A team. Wednesday's Trevor Braithwaite put it this way: 'While I can confidently say that Frank didn't play for our first team, I couldn't tell you definitively that he was or he wasn't on the books of Sheffield Wednesday.'[45] Certainly there is no evidence that Frank Sugg was ever captain of Sheffield Wednesday.

Frank Sugg's move to a position with Derbyshire County Cricket Club in the summer of 1884 coincided with the establishment of Derby County Football Club as an offshoot of the cricket club. (It was hoped that football matches on the county ground would help

---

42 Brian Bearshaw, *From The Stretford End, the Official History of Lancashire CCC*, Partridge Press, 1990, p 110.

43 *Wisden*, 1934.

44 R.A.Sparling, *The Romance of the Wednesday* (Facsimile Edition), Desert Island Books, 1997, p 53.

45 Email, 5 January 2009. See also Tony Matthews, *The Men Who Made Sheffield Wednesday FC*, Stadia Books, 2007. This lists all Sheffield Wednesday players between 1880 and 2007. Frank Sugg does not appear.

to improve the cricket club's precarious financial position.) Sugg played in Derby County's third match of the 1884 season against Notts County at Trent Bridge, Derby losing 3-1. But Derby County's archives do not include complete records for pre-1888 appearances. Among the known facts are that Frank has the distinction of scoring the first hat-trick for County in a competitive match (against Stafford Road on 15 November 1884) and that he played in Derby County's first-ever FA Cup tie in the same year, on 8 November, when County suffered a 7-0 defeat at the hands of Walsall.[46] Apart from these, it seems that Frank's appearances were in 'friendlies' or minor matches, though it should be added that a 'friendly' before the onset of organised Football League matches could still involve games with other leading clubs. There is no evidence that Frank Sugg was captain of Derby County.

An earlier chapter has described how Frank Sugg came to move from his position at Derby to one at Burnley where he had a secretarial position and played both cricket and football for the Burnley club. Once again, there are no comprehensive statistics on Frank's appearances for the football club but his first known match was on 21 September 1885, when he scored one goal in Burnley's easy 9-0 win against Derby St Luke's at Turf Moor. He appeared in three FA Cup ties for Burnley, on 23 October 1886 in a 3-3 draw against Astley Bridge, on 15 October 1887 in a 4-0 victory against Darwen Old Wanderers and on 5 November 1886 against Accrington when Burnley lost 2-3. His versatility is demonstrated by appearances at centre-forward, centre- or wing-half and even, occasionally, in goal. His popularity at Burnley Football Club was recognised when Albert Craig, the 'Surrey rhymester', who in the thirty years before the First World War made a living by writing and selling verses about the celebrated cricketers and footballers of his time, wrote a rhyme about Frank with the title, *Good Lad Frank.* Here is one of its four verses:

> Frank puts his whole heart in the business
> That's the reason he is prized by all
> He's a champion centre-half back,
> And most brilliant at kicking at goal.
> He's genial and kind in manner
> And always in thorough good trim.

---

46 See Anton Rippon and Andrew Ward, *The Story of Derby County, 1884–1991*, Breedon Books, 1991.

And 'tis said he's most fond of Burnley,
And Burnley is fond of him.[47]

Apparently Frank Sugg did captain Burnley, but only on a temporary basis when the regular captain was unavailable. In January 1888, Frank was suspended for a month for failing to turn up for training and soon after his return to duty the club, notwithstanding any mutual fondness, decided to dispense with his services.[48]

According to Burnley Football Club's historian, after Frank left that club he played for Bolton Wanderers. Yet in answer to my request for information, the Bolton club said: 'We have no record of Frank Sugg having played for us. He may have appeared as a guest in a reserve game, but he certainly has not appeared in a competitive first-team game.'[49] There is more solid information on Frank Sugg's appearances for Everton. He played for the club between 1888, the year in which the Football League was established, and 1890. Sugg made ten appearances in the Everton first team in League matches - his only matches in the Football League - and doubtless also turned out for the club in more minor fixtures.[50] These appearances mark Frank Sugg as one of those who played professional cricket and football at the highest level. But whereas Frank was an established county cricketer and had been capped by England, his future in professional football would have appeared more limited. It was probably not surprising that, after the 1890 season, Frank should learn that his services were no longer required by Everton.

Frank played for football clubs big and small.

As well as the clubs mentioned above, all of which are significant football clubs in the present day, Frank played for a

47 For an attractive and informative biography of Craig, see Tony Laughton, *Captain of the Crowd: Albert Craig, Cricket and Football Rhymester, 1849-1909*, Boundary Books, 2008. The rhyme on Frank Sugg the footballer is not mentioned in the book. Lorna Brown provided me with a copy of it.

48 The writer is grateful to Ray Simpson, historian of Burnley Football Club, for much of the information in this paragraph.

49 Email, 7 May 2009.

50 His final season appears to have been 1892 when he played for West Manchester.

variety of other sides, notably his local side Southport Central, later to become Southport Football Club. After leaving Everton he was still young, fit and keen enough to continue to play for various club sides in local leagues for a number of further seasons. He also assisted, off the field, in various capacities. Thus, in a history of the Southport club, we read that on 3 March 1891, when Southport visited Bootle to play an inaugural match under floodlights, the lights 'were under the managership of Central defender Frank Sugg, a former Everton and Derby County footballer and a County Cricketer.'[51]

We can be sure that Frank would have given one hundred per cent on behalf of any club of which he was a member, whether off the field or on it. As a player, his commitment was never in doubt. His height and strength made him a formidable opponent. One contemporary match report confirms that Frank Sugg was not one to hold back when tempers flared. In a match between Notts County and Everton in November 1888, 'one or two of the Everton team played very hard on their opponents, and hoots and groans were frequent during the match.' When the players left the field, spectators rushed to attack the Everton players, one of whom was felled by a blow from a heavy stick. Sugg waded into the melée and grasped the assailant but he wriggled free before the attending policemen could get to the scene.[52]

Frank's involvement with several of the leading football clubs of his day added to his stature as a professional sportsman and would have been of considerable commercial value to the sports business he had founded (with his brother) in 1888, if only for publicity and advertising purposes. In its beginning, the business concentrated on cricket equipment and clothing, but, as we shall see in a later chapter, it soon branched out into the requisites of other sports, including football. The Sugg brand became widely known, and the Sugg products were endorsed by leading sportsmen of the day. Just as in the early days of the business when Frank made use of his acquaintances in the world of cricket, later he drew on his contacts in football. For example, after the First World War, when his business was in difficulties, he persuaded Mr R.Clayton, the chairman of Everton Football Club, to take on its chairmanship.

---

51 From Geoff Wilde's History of Southport FC, at www.southportfootballclub.co.uk/home/summary.php/season

52 *Sporting Chronicle*, 19 November 1888.

If the picture conveyed by references to Sugg the footballer in the cricket literature is somewhat misleading, or risks being so, it needs to be remembered that Frank Sugg's appearances for his various football clubs were in the years before the Football League was established and nationally organised competitive fixtures were put in place. There is therefore only patchy information on Frank's football career in these years. Most of the matches in which he played were 'friendlies' about which there is limited accessible information. The various cricket writers may have relied on one source, Frank Sugg himself. In a profile based on a conversation with Frank Sugg in *Cricket*, 23 April 1896, W.A.Bettesworth reported: 'He played centre forward for Sheffield Wednesday and captained the team. Afterwards he was captain of Derby County when the club was just beginning its career. Again, as centre half back, he captained Burnley and finally was in the Bolton Wanderers' team in the same position.' Could it be that Sugg, looking back a few years after he had hung up his football boots, exaggerated the role he played with these clubs, knowingly or not, and that that exaggeration has been carried forward by subsequent writers and, eventually, into his *Wisden* obituary?[53]

53 While this book was at the printers, an article by Ken Grime on Lancashire's cricketing footballers was published in the *Lancashire Cricket Yearbook*, 2011. It covers similar ground to the chapter above, if more briefly, and reaches the same conclusion, that Frank Sugg's involvement with various football clubs may not have been as significant as cricket histories have suggested.

Chapter Six
Early Seasons with Lancashire

While Frank Sugg was employed by Burnley and in the process of qualifying by residence to play for the county, the Lancashire committee was searching for ways to strengthen the county side, especially in batting. Formed in 1864, the early years of the Lancashire county club were difficult ones but by the late 1870s Lancashire had become one of the country's leading county sides. In 1879, they shared the Championship with Nottinghamshire and in 1881 went one better in winning the title outright for the first time, albeit with Notts weakened by a players' strike. In 1882 they were again joint champions with Nottinghamshire. In A.N.Hornby, Lancashire had an inspiring captain (from 1880) and one of the finest batsmen in the land. Other outstanding players in these years were R.G. ('Dickie') Barlow (the only Lancashire-born professional), Alec Watson, A.G.Steel (the most celebrated of the four Steel brothers who played for the county), Walter Robinson, Johnny Briggs (perhaps Lancashire's outstanding allrounder of all time)[54] and Jack Crossland (the fast bowler whose career with Lancashire was to be mired in controversy over the legitimacy of his action and his residential qualification to play for the county).

But after 1882 Lancashire's performances fell away, especially in the batting department. The committee did not shrink from blooding newcomers but few were able to seize their opportunity: in 1883 there were 13 and in 1885 no fewer than 15 debutants, but as Peter Wynne-Thomas tartly observed, 'most were of little more than passing interest.'[55] Lancashire's needs were compounded by the frequent non-availability of A.G.Steel and other amateurs, and the prospective retirement of the professional batsman, Walter Robinson. Hence the opportunity to hire Frank Sugg, with four years' experience of county cricket behind him, was heaven-sent. And Frank had no hesitation in accepting Lancashire's terms – £5 a

---

54 Despite never achieving the double.
55 Peter Wynne-Thomas, *The History of Lancashire County Cricket Club*, Christopher Helm, 1989, p 44.

match plus a sovereign for a win at home and an extra £1 for away matches - and the chance to revive his cricket career. With its ground at Old Trafford one of the country's leading venues, a hinterland of thriving local cricket clubs and leagues to draw on, and support that was the envy of most counties, there was no reason to doubt that Lancashire would soon regain a position of prominence in county cricket.

Wisden's comment on Lancashire's acquisition was perceptive: 'With a fine natural style and great power, he should render his latest employer great service but his inability to play a steady game detracts in some degree from his usefulness.'[56] Frank, who never received any coaching, had a simple approach to batting: 'Of course, my play was not a model of consistency. I never aimed at staying in to potter about. I looked upon the argument between a batsman and a bowler this way: if you did not knock him off, he would knock you out. Make a man think he can't bowl. That was my motto.'[57] His trademark shots were expansive drives down the ground and pulls to leg, though once set he could display a wider repertoire of strokes. His approach made him a great favourite with the crowds who anticipated some big hitting whenever he came to the crease. Although his captains would often rue Sugg's reluctance to develop the defensive side of the batsman's art and 'get his head down' at the beginning of an innings, his aggression on under-prepared and spiteful wickets, in particular, could be more effective than the more circumspect style of others. And, aside from his runs, in taking the fight to the opposition, his powerful hitting could have an uplifting effect on the morale of his side.

When Frank finally came to make his debut for Lancashire, against MCC at Lord's, he was bowled by W.G.Grace for only seven runs in the first innings and he was out for the same score when the county batted again in a match that Lancashire won by two wickets. This must have been a disappointing start but Frank appeared in all seven of Lancashire's remaining matches in the Championship, usually batting at first wicket down. It was thanks to much improved batting that Lancashire finished second to Surrey in 1887. Sugg made a useful contribution, totalling 417 runs in his eight matches at an average of 29.75, third behind Walter Robinson and Joseph Eccles, the county's leading

56 *Wisden*, 1888, p 36.
57 *Sporting Chronicle*, 25 July 1916.

run-scorer that season. Sugg's highest score was 98 against Surrey at Kennington Oval where he and Eccles put on 152 in an hour and fifty minutes. Sugg was also called upon to bowl a few overs in 1887 and against Gloucestershire he took two for 20 runs off eight overs of his 'slows', both victims caught and bowled. Despite the inconsistency of his batting, Frank Sugg had quickly established himself as an important member of the Lancashire side.

The 1888 season saw the visit of the sixth Australian side to tour England. In Australia the side was not regarded as truly representative of the 'colony' in view of the absence, for one reason or another, of F.R.Spofforth, H.Moses, T.P.Horan and George Giffen. Three preparatory matches had been lost before the team set sail on 24 March. The party, which consisted of only thirteen players, nevertheless included some excellent cricketers, including the captain and opening batsman Percy McDonnell, on his fourth tour of England; the stalwarts Bannerman and wicketkeeper Blackham, who had been on all five previous tours; the big-hitting Bonnor; the impressive allrounder S.P.Jones; another demon bowler in C.T.B.Turner; and the talented young left-armer J.J.Ferris. The tour was to be an arduous one, stretching over four months with no fewer than forty matches. As well as three Tests and matches against the counties, fixtures with a variety of invitation elevens of mixed quality were arranged, the aim, no doubt, being to boost the tour finances. The tourists did not leave for home until 12 October. A modern-day cricketer would be staggered at the thought of such a programme and length of time away from home.

The Australians' visit was eagerly anticipated by English followers of the game and by those cricketers who had hopes of being selected for the Tests. Frank Sugg could hardly have expected to make the Test side. His immediate aim was to consolidate his position as one of Lancashire's leading batsmen. His season started slowly. After scoring only six and two in Lancashire's opening fixture against Kent, he missed a number of games through injury, a rare occurrence in his career. The second match on his return was at Gloucester's Spa Ground played on an under-prepared pitch full of weeds. After Gloucestershire were bowled out for 48, Barlow taking five for 13, Lancashire struggled to 232 for eight by the close of play on the first day. Sugg had made a blistering and unbeaten 102 out of 173 runs scored while he was at the crease. Rain washed out play on the final two days but Frank could take pleasure from scoring his first hundred for Lancashire (and second in first-class cricket) and in such demanding conditions and circumstances.

The bad weather was to ruin many a match in this season: 'pitiful wet' was one paper's description of the summer. With wickets uncovered and often ill-prepared, conditions in 1888 generally favoured bowlers and help to explain why many batsmen, Sugg included, failed to match their performances of the previous season. But his hundred at Gloucester put Frank Sugg into the public eye; and of course the innings was witnessed at first hand by W.G.Grace who was to captain England later in the season. After a couple more matches for Lancashire in one of which, against Oxford University, he scored 58 runs, Frank Sugg was chosen to play for the North of England against the Australians at Old Trafford. The North side consisted of players from Lancashire and Nottinghamshire only as Yorkshire had a clashing fixture but was still strong enough to give the Australians a hard game, the visitors winning by five wickets with ten minutes to spare. In the North's first innings of 93, Sugg scored 27 and figured in an important partnership of 49 for the sixth wicket with Barlow when, in the words of one report, 'his cricket - invaluable in its way - was a contrast to that of his partner'. It was assumed that readers would know that Barlow played a stonewalling role. In the North's second innings, Sugg scored 24 out of his side's 96, again figuring in a useful partnership with Barlow after the North had lost their first five wickets for 14. In helpful conditions, Turner and Ferris took 19 wickets between them in the match. Sugg had shown that he could hold his own against the Australians' two star bowlers.

After this match, and before the team for the First Test match at Lord's was to be announced on 10 July, Lancashire had two county matches but Sugg failed to score in his one innings against Yorkshire and made only 16 in the one innings he had against Middlesex. It would have been no surprise that his name was not among the eleven chosen, by a sub-committee of MCC, to represent England in the Test. The eleven comprised four amateurs W.G.Grace, A.G.Steel, J.Shuter and W.W.Read; and seven professionals, W.Barnes, W.Gunn, W.Attewell, M.Sherwin, J.Briggs, R.Peel and G.A.Lohmann. Last-minute changes were made however: Bobby Abel, whose omission in the first place had been roundly criticised, replaced Shuter when he became unavailable, and it was decided that Attewell could be released in view of the side's bowling strength and be replaced by a batsman. According to the usually well-informed *Cricket*, 'had time allowed, in all probability, Sugg would, we understand, have been played but Mr T.C.O'Brien, being available and on the spot was utilised to fill Attewell's place.'[58] *Cricket* does not say how Attewell reacted to his last-minute rejection. Nor does the magazine's writer comment further on his insight into the possible selection of Frank Sugg. It would certainly have come as a surprise to most cricket followers.

The Australians had started their tour in fine style with five successive wins before being defeated by Lancashire at Old Trafford, one of the matches which Frank Sugg had to miss, when, needing only 90 to win in their second innings, the visitors were bowled out for 66 with Briggs taking five for 15 and the Rev J.R.Napier, on his debut, four for 18. Later in the season the cleric was to take four for 0 against Yorkshire at Bramall Lane and he appeared to be the answer to Lancashire's prayer for a new fast bowler, but these were to be the only first-class matches in which he played. By the time of the First Test the Australians had played 20 matches (again quite extraordinary to a contemporary observer), won 13, drawn three and lost four. They had lost the services of S.P.Jones who had fallen seriously ill early in the tour and who played little further part in it. The Australians won a low-scoring match played on another damp and difficult wicket by 61 runs, with Turner and Ferris, as so often on the tour, the match winners, taking eighteen of the England wickets between them. This was only the second victory of an Australian side in England, the other being the victory at The Oval in 1882 which led to the famous mock obituary in *The Sporting Times* and thereby to the birth of The Ashes. England's defeat in 1888 was not marked so dramatically but was a considerable shock nevertheless.

Immediately before the First Test, Frank Sugg played at The Oval in the second of the season's Gentlemen v Players matches. It was the most significant representative match in which he had appeared so far in his career, for the fixtures were the most prestigious after Test matches. The match was something of a farce however, being practically finished in a single day. Rain prevented any play on the first day. On the second day, the strong Players side scored 176, of which Sugg, batting at number six and playing 'good cricket', made 28, the second top-score to Johnny Briggs' 29, and then dismissed

58 *Cricket*, 19 July 1888.

the Gentlemen for 76 and 61, needing only half an hour on the final morning to finish the job. Peel and Barnes in the Gentlemen's first innings, and Lohmann and Briggs in the second, were the Players' chief destroyers. In the words of one report, 'the Gentlemen's play was quite unworthy of the occasion'. But Frank Sugg could feel that he had again made a useful mark in difficult batting conditions in a match that mattered and, with England about to fail in the First Test, the timing could not have been more helpful.

Meanwhile the County Championship was well under way. Lancashire had won two and lost only one of their first six matches, putting them in second place to unbeaten Surrey. Between the end of the First Test and the date when the team for the Second Test at Kennington Oval would be announced, Sugg played in three county matches for Lancashire. As so often in that dreadful summer, all were affected by rain and the damaged wickets made batting difficult. In the first of the three, against Yorkshire at Old Trafford, Lancashire were all out for 79 in their first innings, Peel taking five for 32. Sugg scored 27 in what *Cricket* described as 'an excellent display in the circumstances'. When Yorkshire batted, Johnny Briggs went one better than his Yorkshire rival spinner, taking six for 24 in the Yorkshire total of only 51. Peel then took seven for 31 as Lancashire were dismissed for 82 in their second innings. After a loss of early wickets Yorkshire eventually scored the 111 needed for victory with two wickets remaining. Briggs had to be content with two for 32 in this innings but the bowling figures are sufficient testimony to the demands made upon the batsmen of both sides. The next match was against Gloucestershire at the Aigburth ground in Liverpool and again the conditions were heavily in favour of the bowlers. Lancashire made 108 in their first knock, to which Frank Sugg contributed only eight, and then dismissed Gloucestershire for a paltry 33, Briggs taking six for 13. In their second innings, Lancashire stumbled to 97, of which Sugg made a belligerent 23, and the visitors were then bowled out for 56, Briggs this time taking six for 32. The third of the three matches brought the unbeaten Surrey side to Old Trafford. The wretched weather ruined what had been expected to be a keenly fought contest. The match was all over in a single day. Lancashire were shot out for 35 and 63, leaving Surrey victors by an innings and 25 runs. George Lohmann took 13 wickets in the day, eight for 13 in Lancashire's first innings. Only four Lancashire batsmen reached double figures in the two innings, the highest score being Frank Sugg's 20 in the second innings.

The Lancashire side of 1888, in sylvan setting.
Standing (l to r): G.R.Baker, F.H.Sugg, F.Taylor, R.G.Barlow, E.E.Steel, G.Yates.
Seated: S.M.Crosfield, A.N.Hornby (capt), R.Pilling (wk), J.Eccles.
On the ground: A.Watson, J.Briggs.

Frank Sugg may not have scored many runs in these matches, but he played some useful innings on spiteful wickets, invariably in his customary aggressive style. His willingness to take the fight to the bowlers when the ball was fizzing and turning in unpredictable ways impressed commentators on the game as well as cricket followers. Before the Surrey county committee met to select the twelve for the Second Test, Frank Sugg played in two matches that were not first-class. Against Cheshire at Old Trafford, mixing big hitting with stylish driving, Frank Sugg made 117 of the Lancashire total of 225, after which the bowling of Briggs and Alec Watson proved far too good for the Cheshire batsmen and Cheshire were easily beaten by an innings and 93 runs. Even if against modest opposition, Frank Sugg's second century of the season was a timely indication of his qualities.

A second match against lesser opposition was more painful for Frank. In late August Lancashire visited Derby to take on the county side in a two-day match, Derbyshire no longer being a first-class county. It was Frank's first visit to the County Ground since he had left the club. Frank's brother Walter scored 48 in Derbyshire's first innings of 171 and at the close of the first day Derbyshire had reduced Lancashire to 103 for seven. Frank, who was booed as he went out to bat, scored only five. After overnight rain, the match swung Lancashire's way when, after reaching 139 in their first innings, they dismissed Derbyshire for only 56, leaving Lancashire needing only 88 to win. The crowd took noisy exception during Derbyshire's innings to some of the umpires' decisions and when Frank went out to join his captain, A.N.Hornby, in the second innings at the fall of Lancashire's first wicket, the noise reached such a pitch that Hornby left the field and threatened to abandon the match. The cricket columnist of *The Derbyshire Times*, while not condoning the crowd's behaviour, commented: 'It was ridiculous to suppose that Frank Sugg's appearance in Derby would create anything but a scene. The circumstances under which he deserted Derbyshire, Mr Hornby's own share in the transaction, and Sugg's peculiar relations with certain Derby people, all these are matters of notoriety in Derbyshire, if not in Lancashire, and, rightly or wrongly a strong feeling of resentment prevails.'[59] In his own (later) comment on the incident, Frank said he urged Hornby to continue with the game as the crowd could not understand his reasons for quitting his home county. Frank continued: 'The first ball after this, I made a very big hit. The ball dropped on the roof of the pavilion and broke a couple of tiles. At this, the crowd, who were really good sportsmen, cheered as vigorously as they had hooted before and after this it was alright.'[60] The crowd may well have cheered the hit, but Frank was not naïve enough to suppose that a good rapport with the crowd had been restored by one big hit. They did cheer when he was out for 15, bowled by John Hulme, Derbyshire's left-arm fast-medium bowler, as he had been in the first innings, but Lancashire proceeded smoothly enough to a four-wicket victory. While Derbyshire might well have felt that Hornby had overreacted

59 *The Derbyshire Times*, 25 August 1888.
60 *Cricket*, 23 April 1896.

on the day, Hornby was so incensed by the crowd's behaviour that he persuaded the Lancashire committee to drop the fixture for the following four seasons.

When the twelve names for the Test were announced, Frank was delighted, and no doubt rather surprised, to learn that his name was among them. Sugg, George Ulyett, John Shuter and Harry Wood replaced O'Brien, Sherwin, Gunn and Steel of the eleven who had played at Lord's. Steel was invited but declined to play. Effectively it was Steel's place that was taken by Sugg, a very different style of cricketer to the haughty amateur. Probably the selectors thought that Sugg's powerful hitting could be just the thing to unsettle Australia's star bowlers, Turner and Ferris. The team therefore comprised three amateurs, W.G.Grace, W.W.Read and J.Shuter; and eight professionals, R.Abel, W.Barnes, J.Briggs, G.A.Lohmann, R.Peel, G.Ulyett, H.Wood and Sugg. The Australians fielded the same side that had triumphed at Lord's. It was their

The England side which defeated Australia at The Oval in August 1888 by an innings and 137 runs.
Standing (l to r): R.Peel, G.A.Lohmann, F.H.Sugg, G.Ulyett.
Seated: J.Shuter, W.Barnes, W.G.Grace (capt), W.W.Read.
On the ground: R.Abel, J.Briggs, H.Wood (wk).
This was Sugg's first Test match.

twenty-ninth match of the tour – it was now mid August – and the Australians were, not surprisingly, showing signs of fatigue.

The Australians batted first and, in splendid conditions for a change, mustered only 80 in their first innings, the batting so tedious at one stage that fourteen successive four-ball maidens were sent down by the England bowlers, Lohmann and Briggs. Briggs had another splendid day, finishing with five for 25 off no fewer than 37 overs with 24 maidens. After a shaky start in which W.G. and Ulyett were out with only six runs on the board, England batted more steadily and eventually posted a first-innings score of 317 with Abel making 70, Barnes 62, Lohmann 62 not out and Sugg, at seven, 31. The ever-persevering Turner bowled 60 overs and finished with six for 112. Frank Sugg had the good fortune to be missed twice in the slips and the misfortune to run out his partner Bobby Abel by calling for 'a stupidly short run'. Sugg 'played very fluky cricket indeed', according to the report in *Wisden.* He was to have no chance of making a better impression as the Australians were dismissed for 100 in their second innings leaving England the winners by an innings and 187 runs in just two days. Percy McDonnell made 32 but no one else had much success in combating the fine bowling of Peel, who took four for 49, and Barnes, five for 32, though Alex Bannerman hung on for an hour and 25 minutes while scoring only five. It was the allround strength of the England attack compared with the Australians' heavy reliance on Charles Turner and, to a lesser extent, John Ferris that proved the main difference between the two sides. 30,957 paying spectators watched the two days' play.

The Third and final Test was to be at Old Trafford and to start on 30 August after the end of the county season. Sugg played in two county matches in the interval between the Tests. The first of these was against Surrey, the championship leaders, who were still unbeaten after eleven matches, at The Oval. It was a triumph for Lancashire. After Surrey had scored a useful 294 in their first innings, Lancashire responded with 376, with Joseph Eccles scoring a magnificent 184 in opening the innings. Sugg contributed only four. Surrey were then put out for 152 and Lancashire knocked off the 71 required for victory for the loss of only one wicket; Sugg, revelling in the favourable situation, finished with 41 not out. However this was only Lancashire's fourth win of what was proving to be a disappointing season, a season in which the wet weather had undoubtedly dealt the northern county a poor hand. The final match of the Championship for Lancashire was against Nottinghamshire at Old Trafford and this finished as a draw, after rain had once again played a malevolent part. During the two days in which play was possible 32 wickets fell for a total of 254 runs: Frank Sugg contributed three and nought in his two excursions to the crease.

Surrey were worthy winners of the Championship with twelve wins from their 14 matches. Lancashire finished a disappointing fifth in *Wisden's* unofficial table, with just four wins from the same number of matches. Joseph Eccles was Lancashire's leading batsman with 525 championship runs at an average of 27.12, followed by Johnny Briggs who had a triumphant season with bat and ball, and then by Frank Sugg. Sugg scored 316 runs in his 20 championship innings at an average of 17.55, boosted, it has to be said, by his 102 not out at Gloucester. Barlow and Hornby had averages of only 15.28 and 15 respectively. For Surrey, six of their regular batsmen had higher averages than Eccles which shows that it was the batting that let Lancashire down, even when allowance is made for the awful weather that summer.

It is fair to add that Sugg's contribution to his side could be more valuable than the statistics might suggest, his hard hitting in useful partnerships after Lancashire had lost early wickets not infrequently helping to stem the tide. The disappointment was that he rarely turned a hard-hit twenty or so into something more substantial. And Sugg continued to be vulnerable early in his innings; in 12 of his 20 championship innings he failed to reach double figures.

Sugg may well have felt he had not done enough to retain his place in the Test side but he had the advantage that the team was to be selected by the Lancashire committee and it was common practice at the time for the selectors to give preference to players of the host county. Lancashire's Richard Pilling was chosen as wicketkeeper in place of Wood and Gunn replaced John Shuter when the Surrey captain declined the invitation to play. Once again, and even though the Test was on his county ground, A.G.Steel could not make himself available. The team was therefore: W.G.Grace, W.W.Read, R.Abel, G.Ulyett, W.Barnes, F.H.Sugg, W.Gunn, R.Peel, J.Briggs, G.A.Lohmann and R.Pilling. After heavy rain in the preceding days, winning the toss was an advantage and it was England who had first use of the wicket. They compiled 172 runs with Sugg joint second top-scorer with 24 behind W.G.'s 38. There was no criticism of Sugg's batting this time: He 'showed really good cricket' in the words of one report. Turner bowled throughout the innings and finished with five for 86 off 59 four-ball overs, another example of his remarkable stamina and at the end of a very long season. In increasingly difficult conditions for batting, Australia were dismissed for 81 and 70, leaving England successful by an innings and 21 runs by lunch time on the second day - when thousands were apparently still streaming to the ground in anticipation of some good cricket. (15,549 spectators paid to watch the one and a bit days' play.) In Australia's first innings Bobby Peel had figures of seven for 31 and he followed this up with another four wickets in the second innings when no fewer than six Australian batsmen failed to score. England therefore took the series and, hypothetically, the Ashes, by two matches to one.

The Australians' tour was not over after this final Test match. They had a further six fixtures to fulfil, beginning with a match at Harrogate against 'An England XI', followed by one match at each of the Scarborough and Hastings cricket festivals, two matches against teams representing Arthur Shrewsbury's side that had toured Australia the previous winter, and then a final and third fixture against Surrey at Kennington Oval. One can imagine how hard it must have been for the tourists to raise enthusiasm for these matches. Frank Sugg was involved only in the match at Harrogate. The England side included several leading players but also two local cricketers. Heavy rain once again delayed the start of the match and the Australians found batting difficult against Briggs and Attewell and were all out for 70. Sugg, opening the innings with his Lancashire teammate Barlow, was clean bowled by Charles Turner for a duck and the England XI could only muster 111. After the Australians had struggled to 168 in their second innings, Turner and Ferris shared nine wickets between them in bowling the Englishmen out for a mere 71, giving the tourists a well-earned victory by 56 runs. Sugg top scored with 18 in this innings 'by good hitting'.

Frank Sugg's season finally came to a close at Hastings in the North v South match. Two evenly matched sides made good use of an excellent wicket, the South winning by 47 runs with only four minutes play remaining. 881 runs were scored in the three days, a high-scoring match compared to most in the 1888 season. Frank Sugg scored eight and 28 in his two innings. His performance was a microcosm of his season: too often was he dismissed early in an innings or, alternatively, after he made a useful start and seemed to have built a platform for a decent score.

Performing rather better in his innings outside the County Championship than he did for Lancashire, in all first-class matches in 1888, Frank Sugg scored 565 runs at an average of 19.48. He did not bowl this season. He had the satisfaction of his two Test appearances but, looking back, he knew that he had not fulfilled the expectations with which he had started the season. There were no more Test matches in England until the next visit of the Australians scheduled for 1890. Frank would, by then, be 28 years old and could expect to be at the peak of his career. Perhaps he would have another chance to establish himself as a Test batsman then. Meanwhile, when the curtain finally came down on the 1888 cricket season, Frank could turn to football and to building up the sports outfitting business he had started with his brother. He was also on the brink of a change in his domestic circumstances.

Chapter Seven
Marriage and Family

Early in 1889 Frank Sugg married. His bride was Amy Alice Smith who lived in the small village of Stonehouse, near Stroud in Gloucestershire. Frank was 27 years old, Amy an attractive young woman of only 17 years. No doubt Frank would have had other female friends, perhaps even other romances, but it was in character for him to have bided his time before embarking on the responsibilities of marriage and of bringing up a family. By 1889 he was a well-established professional cricketer with two England caps already to his name, and with worthwhile achievements in other sports. Moreover, in partnership with his brother he had started his sports business the previous year and he had every reason to expect that this would prosper and provide financial security in the coming years. It was a good stage in his life to be

St Cyr's Church, Stonehouse in 2010.
Frank Sugg married Amy Smith here in 1889.

looking for a wife. The surprise is that his choice fell upon a young girl – a minor – who lived a long way from Frank's base in Liverpool, though we should remember that it was not all that unusual in Victorian times for men to marry much younger women.

As to how the couple came to meet, a contemporary source suggests that it was at a county cricket match: 'It was as a representative of Lancashire that Sugg discovered his wife as she admired his play in Brighton where Lancashire were playing Sussex in 1888.'[61] This cannot be correct. Lancashire did indeed play Sussex at Hove[62] in 1888, but Frank was not in the team. He could not have been a 'representative of Lancashire' in any other capacity as, on the days of the match, Frank Sugg was appearing for England against the Australians at Kennington Oval. Certainly Lancashire would have liked Sugg to be in their team because they were emphatically beaten by nine wickets inside two days, having at one stage in their first innings been 28 for seven wickets.

It is possible that the date is wrong in this account. Sugg certainly played in the corresponding fixture in 1887, the match starting on 22 August, and he acquitted himself well in Lancashire's victory by four wickets. He scored 69 runs in each of Lancashire's innings, top-scoring in the first, and in the Sussex second innings bowled a few overs and took a couple of catches. Frank was therefore prominent throughout the match and, handsome and athletic as he was, he could well have caught the eye of a young female spectator. If Amy was a spectator, it was no doubt with family members during a seaside holiday. But Amy was only 15 years old at the time of this game and it is hard to believe that any admiration that she may have felt for Frank or for his play in it could have led directly to a romance between the two.

If Amy had an interest in cricket, it is possible that she was among the spectators at Gloucester, close to her home, in June 1888 when Lancashire were the visitors and when Frank scored a whirlwind 102 not out in the single day on which play was possible, and that it was at this match that Frank first met his future wife. If this were the beginning of the relationship, the courtship would have been a

61 Joseph Stoddart, *Men I Have Met*, p 61.

62 The Sussex ground was at Hove, but was often identified as Brighton at the time, though that is of no consequence in this context.

whirlwind affair since the wedding took place only a few months later.

Anyhow, whatever the date on which the couple first met, Frank was able, between his various cricket and business commitments, to meet Amy and her family enough times to satisfy himself that she was the wife for him and, more to the point, to satisfy Amy's father, George Smith, a businessman in the woollen textiles industry, that he had the means adequately to support her. In consenting to the marriage of his 17-year-old daughter, Mr Smith must have been impressed by Frank's qualities and prospects.

The wedding was in the bride's parish church, St Cyr's at Stonehouse, with Frank's brother Walter the best man. After the reception, the bride's father provided a spectacular firework display to celebrate the occasion and the whole village was 'quite en fete'. After a honeymoon in London, the couple made their first home in rural North Meols, near Southport in West Lancashire. They lived in Southport for much of Frank's first-class cricket career, but around the turn of the century, they moved to Walton, by now one of Liverpool's sprawling suburbs, perhaps so that Frank could be closer to his place of business in the centre of town. The Suggs lived at 2 Albert Drive,[63] a substantial brick-built property on a corner plot, these days converted into flats. While many Victorian properties remain in the area, the extensive rebuilding of this part of Liverpool would make it unrecognisable to the Suggs.

The Suggs moved out of Liverpool at some point, probably after the First World War, to Waterloo, a district of the present Liverpool conurbation, between Bootle and Crosby. Their final home was at 65 St Johns Road, one of a terrace of once elegant brick-built, three-storeyed houses. The ground floors of almost all these houses are now lock-up shops; No.65 is a haberdasher's.

It was some time before the Suggs' first child arrived but in December 1895 Amy gave birth, in Southport, to a son whom they christened Frank Reginald. The son did not share his father's interest in, and talent at, sports. No doubt this was some disappointment to Frank. But Frank Reginald had other talents. He was a fine singer (he once sang in the Royal Albert Hall with Queen Alexandra among the audience) and an accomplished pianist and

---

63 The 1911 census has the Sugg family living at this address.

organist. Frank senior might have had plans for Frank Reginald to be actively involved in his growing sports business once his schooling, at Merchant Taylors' School at Great Crosby just outside Liverpool, was out of the way. If so, these expectations were soon put aside. In due course, the young man had shares in the business and, as we shall see in a later chapter, he had an influence in a key decision that led to the splitting of the company into two separate businesses. But he had no active and continuing role in Frank's business. The reins of the business remained firmly in the hands of Frank and his brother Walter until its collapse in the mid 1920s. After service in France during the First World War, Frank Reginald joined the civil service. He worked in the Newcastle offices of the Ministry of Labour and on retirement moved to the Isle of Wight.

For a brief period, including while he was in the Army, Frank Reginald chose to be known as Frank Reginald Howe-Sugg. I have not been able to discover the reason. Perhaps by incorporating his father's second forename into his own surname, Frank Reginald wanted to associate himself more closely with his father and perhaps distance himself from Walter Sugg's branch of the family, with whom his father's relationships were not of the happiest. But that is speculation.

After the death of his first wife, Frank Reginald married Mabel Coleman, who had been his housekeeper, in 1919 in Tynemouth. Both marriages were childless so the male line of Frank's branch of the family was extinguished on Frank Reginald's own death in 1963.

Frank and Amy Sugg also had three daughters, all born in Liverpool: Margery Helen Mary, in 1900; Eva Kathleen, in 1906; and Amy Winifred Howe, in 1910. All married in due course, Margery (known as Margot in the family) and Eva (known as Kath) having families of their own. Kath and her husband Richard Tippin had two daughters, Janet and Lorna. Lorna, born in Harrogate but brought up in Sheffield, married John Hawksley-Wood. The marriage failed and in 1971 she was remarried to Tom Brown, a businessman in the pharmaceutical industry. Widowed, she now lives near Dover. She has been a useful source of information about her grandfather.

Lorna Brown has told me that her mother and her mother's sisters all revered Frank. 'I never heard a bad word said about him in the family,' she told me. Frank was able to provide a comfortable and secure environment for his children. 'It was a happy family and the children were happy in each other's company,' said Lorna. Frank made sure that the girls, as well as their brother Frank Reginald, had a good education 'to fit them for life in the wider world'. In contrast to their brother, the girls were all keen on sports, particularly tennis and swimming. Frank encouraged their interest in every way that he could. During holidays from school in the Isle of Man, Frank would join his children in swimming and rowing.

Frank became interested in art. He was a serious collector of paintings and glassware in particular, though sometimes the lure of profit would tempt him into a quick resale. Landscapes and still lives purchased by Frank are among Lorna's treasured possessions. Frank was also an early enthusiast for motor cars. Perhaps predictably, he got a number of tickets for speeding. On one occasion, a car in which he was travelling, but not driving, overturned. Frank was pinned underneath and unconscious for a few moments. Happily he suffered no serious injury. The newspaper account of the accident reports that the car was 'capable of 40 mph!'[64]

Frank Sugg was very close to his brother, Walter. After all, they ran a successful business together. But it seems that Frank was not popular with Walter's family. Walter's great-grandson, Hubert Henri Timothy Sugg, told me that his grandfather and father, who in their turn had built up their own business, HHB Sugg Ltd, in competition with Frank Sugg's company, regarded Frank as 'the black sheep of the family'. Timothy had no direct knowledge of how this situation had come about. It could have been a result of disputes over business matters but Timothy believes that a more likely cause was Frank's involvement in horse racing (about which more in a later chapter) and in particular his (alleged) gambling habit. Timothy has no direct evidence that Frank was a gambler; it is known that Frank was a keen card player for 'nice fat kitties', though that hardly makes him a compulsive gambler. But gambling was much frowned upon by Timothy Sugg's father and grandfather. Timothy said that both reacted angrily if any conversation strayed on to horse racing, commenting that Frank had 'lost a fortune on the horses', and 'they would not hear his name spoken in the house'. The hostility of Bert Sugg (Timothy's

64 Lorna Brown cutting.

grandfather) and Bert's first wife Evelyn was apparently so deep that Evelyn would not keep any family papers or photographs in which Frank Sugg featured.

It has to be said that Lorna Brown had never heard any suggestion that Frank, her grandfather, had a weakness for gambling. (She had never met Timothy Sugg, who lives in the Hope Valley in Derbyshire, nor any of Timothy's side of the family.) She knew about the financial difficulties that Frank had faced at various times in his life but not of any gambling losses that might have been a contributory factor. It is not possible to establish the facts at this distance but clearly there had to be a serious breakdown in relationships for a man of Frank Sugg's stature to be ostracised by the family of his own brother. However, whatever the cause, it had no bearing on Frank Sugg's cricket career.

Chapter Eight
Lancashire Stalwart

The Lancashire committee took further steps to strengthen the side for the 1889 season with the recruitment of two batsmen, Albert Ward and Arthur Paul, and the fast bowler Arthur Mold, none of whom were born in the county. All were quality players, Ward and Mold both later to play for England. The addition of a fast bowler of Mold's ability, perhaps the fastest bowler in the country on his day - albeit with an action not entirely beyond suspicion - gave a cutting edge to an attack that hitherto had been too dependent on Johnny Briggs and Alec Watson. Briggs took 140 wickets at 11.75 in 1889, Mold 102 at 11.83 and Watson 90 at 12.65, the three occupying second, third and fourth places in the first-class bowling averages. This was the main reason for Lancashire's much better performance in the Championship. They won ten of their 14 matches and shared the title with Surrey and Nottinghamshire, under the points system devised by the Cricket Reporting Agency.

Buoyed by his two Test appearances, Frank Sugg also enjoyed a more successful season than in 1888. He played in all 14 matches in the County Championship, scoring 578 runs and topping the Lancashire averages with 32.11. He played in another six first-class matches, his total of runs in the season being 747 at an average of 27.67. Of his Lancashire colleagues, only Ward outscored him with a total of 822 in all first-class matches at an average of 30.44. Ward's solid batting was a major contributor to Lancashire's success in 1889. During the match late in the season at Kennington Oval, when Lancashire beat their rivals Surrey for the second time in the season, Frank Sugg reached the milestone of 3,000 runs in first-class cricket. He also had the satisfaction of steering Lancashire home with an innings of 44 not out after, needing only 72 runs for victory in their second innings, Lancashire had lost their first two wickets for only five runs. Yet Sugg did not reach three figures in any of his innings in 1889, his top score being 89 for the North against the South at Old Trafford, the benefit match for Lancashire's wicketkeeper Richard Pilling. In this innings, Sugg showed he could temper aggression with patience when there was the need. The North had lost three wickets for only nine runs in reply to the South's first innings of 204, but Frank pulled the innings round in stands first with Gunn and then with Briggs, the North eventually totalling 271 before going on to win by four wickets. While he had not conquered his weakness for getting out early in his innings, in 1889 he was less frequently dismissed for a single-figure score than in previous seasons. It was this improved aspect of his batting which lifted his average to a respectable level.

Although he appeared in both North v South matches, Frank Sugg would have been disappointed not to be selected for the Players in either of the more prestigious Gentlemen v Players matches in 1889. These omissions suggested that he was slipping down the merit table in the selectors' eyes. However, he had the honour of being one of the 1890 *Wisden*'s 'Nine Great Batsmen of the Year'. It was, though, based on performances of the previous season,[65] and the selection was restricted to professionals: any England side of the time would include a number of the leading amateur batsmen. The mixed feelings about Sugg's qualities are reflected in *Wisden*'s citation. It applauded his ability to turn a game by his big hitting but added: 'That he depends more upon quickness of sight than upon a scientific method can easily be seen from the faulty way in which he will often commence an innings on even the best of grounds.' As already noted, Frank would have responded that this was the way he played and that was that.

Lancashire had hopes of winning the Championship in 1890, now played under a formula devised by the counties themselves, but the side was weakened by the absence of Briggs, for a month, and his business partner Pilling, for the whole season, through tuberculosis. (He died the following year, aged only 35.) In the event Lancashire finished second to Surrey with seven wins from their 14 games compared with Surrey's nine. This season Surrey turned the tables on Lancashire by winning both their matches against the northerners; these losses were particularly critical because under the new tariff, a point was deducted from the losers' total for each defeat. Late in the season A.C.MacLaren made his first appearance for Lancashire, soon after he had captained Harrow in the annual fixture against Eton. Archie MacLaren

65 The Almanack had established the practice of honouring players in this fashion only in the previous year's edition when six 'Great Bowlers' were named.

celebrated his debut with a century and was marked down as a future Lancashire captain.

The Australians toured again in 1890, under the captaincy of W.L.Murdoch. The first of three Tests was at Lord's, scheduled to start on 21 July. If Frank Sugg was to have any chance of getting another cap, he needed some big scores early in the season. He scored a fine 66 in Lancashire's second match against Kent and in the county's fourth match against Oxford University he scored 171, his third first-class century, out of Lancashire's total of 475, and followed with 69 in Lancashire's second innings. But otherwise decent scores eluded him in the weeks before the start of the Test series, including Lancashire's match against the tourists. Low points were a pair against Surrey and another against Middlesex, both at Old Trafford. Perhaps surprisingly, he was selected for both the Gentlemen v Players matches, two curtain-raisers for the Tests, although not for the Players match against the Australians that was sandwiched between them. Sadly for Frank's hopes, he failed in both matches; opening with Arthur Shrewsbury each time, he was out for two and three in the first match at Lord's and for nought and six in the second match at Kennington Oval. It was surely no surprise therefore that he was not selected for the First Test at Lord's, commencing on 21 July, which England won comfortably by seven wickets.

For the Second Test at Kennington Oval three weeks later, Attewell and Briggs were unfit and England were further weakened when Yorkshire, due to play Middlesex at Bradford, refused to release Ulyett and Peel; A.E.Stoddart was then withdrawn by Middlesex. James Cranston, the Gloucestershire allrounder, and the pace bowlers J.W.Sharpe and Fred Martin all made their England debuts in this Test. England won a closely fought, low-scoring match by two wickets in two days. 22 wickets fell for 197 runs on the first day, and Martin, the Kent left-armer, took five for 50 and five for 52 in the match.

The final Test was scheduled for Old Trafford, on 25 to 27 August. Frank Sugg did little of note for his county in the run-up to this match, his best score in the preceding three championship matches being 28 against Surrey at Kennington Oval. Nevertheless, Sugg was among the twelve named for the Test. With Ulyett and Peel not considered and the three debutants in the Second Test all discarded, the twelve were W.G.Grace, W.W.Read, A.E.Stoddart, G.MacGregor, A.Shrewsbury, W.Gunn, W.Attewell, G.A.Lohmann,

J.M.Read, J.Briggs, A.W.Mold and Frank Sugg, the final choice to be between Mold and Sugg. Sugg's inclusion, and indeed that of Mold in place of Martin, smacks of bias by the Lancashire selection committee which no doubt foresaw benefits at the gate from the inclusion of some leading Lancashire players. After the first day's play was abandoned because of rain, the *Manchester Guardian* speculated that Mold would be left out because of the sodden conditions; had Mold played, it would have been his first appearance for England.[66] In the event, the match was a complete washout with not a single ball bowled, and with the rain went any opportunity for Frank Sugg to extend his Test career.

After this rain-ruined fixture, Sugg played for the North against the Australians at Headingley and for the North against the South at Hastings, without achieving much in either match. At the very end of the season, he was one of a strong England XI, captained by George Ulyett, against the Australians at Old Trafford. The Australians scored 234 in their first innings, J.E.Barrett

This team, representing the North, lost to the South by nine runs at Hastings in September 1890.
Standing (l to r): F.R.Spofforth, L.Hall, F.H.Sugg, A.Ward.
Seated: G.Ulyett, M.Sherwin (wk), C.W.Wright (capt), W.Gunn, W.Attewell.
On the ground: R.Peel, J.Briggs.
Moustaches de rigeur.

66 Mold was to play in three Tests for England, all in 1893.

top-scoring with 97, and the England XI replied with 167, of which Sugg, batting at eight, scored 31. In their second innings the Australians were 186 for four when the match fizzled out into a draw. This was to prove the closest that Frank Sugg came to appearing again for England against Australia.

All in all, 1890 had turned out to be a disappointing season for Frank Sugg. In all first-class matches he scored 796 runs at an average of 21.51, boosted by his 171 against Oxford, and well down on the previous season. He appeared in 13 of Lancashire's 14 championship matches, scoring 420 runs at an average of 21.00, well down the Lancashire list.

By 1891 progress in Frank Sugg's cricket career appeared to have levelled off. His only first-class cricket that season was for Lancashire. He appeared in 15 of the 16 championship matches and also against MCC and twice against Oxford University. He was not chosen either for the North in the two matches against the South or for the professionals in the two Gentlemen v Players matches, and it was to be the same in the following 1892 season. In his 18 matches in 1891 Frank Sugg scored 557 runs at 21.42 and he finished well down both the national and the Lancashire averages. His highest score was 75, which he achieved twice, against Yorkshire and against Sussex, both in matches which Lancashire won handsomely by an innings. Lancashire's leading batsman in 1891 was again Albert Ward (though Archie MacLaren and A.G.Steel had better averages, they each played only a handful of games) and newcomers George Baker and Arthur Smith also finished above Sugg in the averages. While Mold and Briggs again had outstanding seasons, Alec Watson was troubled by injury and was not the force in 1891 that he had been previously.

Lancashire finished second to Surrey in the County Championship in 1891. This was a satisfactory outcome considering the poor start they made to the season. In the end they won eight of their 16 matches compared to Surrey's 12. There was no disputing Surrey's right to the title once more. Changes in the Lancashire old guard were afoot in 1891. A.N.Hornby played only occasionally, S.M.Crosfield taking over the captaincy when he was not available, and Richard Barlow played his last game for the county, indeed his last first-class match, in 1891, ending a career that extended over twenty seasons.

Sugg was not a serious candidate for Lord Sheffield's party that toured Australia in 1891/92 under the captaincy of W.G.Grace, losing the series by two Test matches to one. Indeed Frank never toured overseas throughout his career. Whether or not his performances ever merited selection, the probability is that his business commitments would have prevented him accepting, had an invitation come his way.

In 1892 Lancashire slipped to fourth in the championship table behind Surrey, Nottinghamshire and Somerset, winning only seven of their 16 matches. Somerset had only become a first-class county the previous year so their third place was commendable. Lancashire had the same personnel to call upon, though Hornby played even fewer games than in the previous season so that Crosfield was effectively, if not officially, the team captain. The bowling remained almost exclusively in the hands of Mold, Briggs and the veteran Watson, with Mold taking 104 wickets at 13.70 in the Championship, Briggs 85 at 13.12 and Watson 52 at 14.25. Extraordinarily, only seven wickets were taken by the other Lancashire bowlers. It was the batting that let the side down in 1892. In Crosfield's words, 'sometimes, for no particular reason, we go to pieces.'[67] As always, this was certainly the case with Frank Sugg, though he did contribute more with the bat than in the previous two seasons. Despite nine innings in which he failed to reach double figures, he scored 705 runs in all first-class matches at an average of 24.31. Sugg played in all 16 championship matches, testimony to his level of fitness, and scored 646 runs at an average of 26. 91. A.P.Smith, Ward and A.C.MacLaren finished above him in the Lancashire averages but by small margins. He made one century in 1892, 107 not out out of 246 against Surrey at Old Trafford. The match was ruined by rain and Frank's innings was spread over all three of the scheduled days - he was 22 not out at the end of the first day and 68 not out at the end of the second - suggesting that he was not always let down by failures in concentration. It is a pity that the weather took the gilt off one of Sugg's better performances.

Frank Sugg's position in the batting order was never firmly fixed, but by 1892 he and Albert Ward were more often than not Lancashire's preferred openers. They made a contrasting pair. Big hitting was still the defining characteristic of Sugg's batting,

---

67 Quoted by Bearshaw, *op.cit.*, p 122.

whereas Ward's was a watchful approach, more in the style of Barlow. Their partnerships did not always last long but when they got established Frank was invariably the main scorer. Typical was the match against Kent at Tonbridge. Sugg and Ward had an opening stand of 87 to which Ward contributed 18, Sugg going on to score 68. Lancashire totalled 484, with G.R.Baker making 109, and won the match by the satisfying margin of an innings and 330 runs. Mold took thirteen wickets, nine for 29 in Kent's second innings of 57 all out, Johnny Briggs predictably taking the remaining wickets save for two run-outs. The match illustrated how formidable Lancashire could be when their batsmen matched the quality performances invariably turned in by their two star bowlers. Commenting on Sugg's season in 1892, *Wisden* said: 'Impatience to score used to be a sad fault in Sugg's batting, but [this] season he appeared to have a much better control over himself and used his brilliant powers as a hitter with much greater discretion.'

The value of Frank Sugg's fielding should not be overlooked. He preferred to field in the deep where his athleticism and powerful arm stood him in good stead but, whether in the deep or close to the wicket, his was a safe pair of hands. In his younger days he was often required to field at long on or long off to both bowlers, prompting the obvious calls 'Get on your bike, Frank.' Sugg liked to tell about his exploits in the field and the many splendid catches that he took. For example, when Dick Lilley of Warwickshire made a big hit, 'I was right on the edge of the boundary, and leaning back to my full reach. I secured the ball just as it was crossing the ropes. Lilley came and shook hands with me for, as a true cricketer, he appreciated the difficulty of the situation.'[68] Of course spectacular fielding was less common then than it is today – as, regrettably, are such sporting gestures as Lilley's. Through most of his career Sugg averaged more than a catch every two matches and in 1892 he accounted for 15 dismissals. In 1897 he was to go one better with 16 catches.

1893 was a better season for Lancashire. Yorkshire topped the table, despite Lord Hawke's absence from ten games, with twelve wins in their 16 matches, and Lancashire were second with nine wins. At least Lancashire had the satisfaction of twice beating their rivals from across the Pennines. The match at Old Trafford in late

68 *Sporting Chronicle*, 1 August 1916.

August, when either county could have gone on to win the Championship, was one of the most thrilling of Roses matches. Before a record crowd of 25,000 on the first day, Lancashire were bowled out for 64 on a treacherous wicket, and Yorkshire in reply for 58, Briggs and Mold, almost as usual, sharing the wickets. Lancashire could only muster 50 in their second innings but with Johnny Briggs on song, Yorkshire were dismissed for 51 in their second innings, leaving Lancashire victorious by five runs. Frank Sugg's contribution in this match was scores of three and nought.

Sugg played in 15 of the 16 championship matches, scoring 858 runs at the excellent average of 34.32, just behind Ward in the Lancashire list. He made three centuries, 169 not out against Sussex, 127 against Nottinghamshire, and 127 against Gloucestershire, and four fifties.

Several of the tallish stories attributed to Frank Sugg involve matches against Gloucestershire. One was in the 1893 match at Old Trafford and, not for the only time, it involved W.G.Grace. When Sugg came to the wicket, Fred Roberts, the Gloucestershire opening bowler, asked for a fielder to be placed on the square-leg boundary. Grace refused, instructing Roberts to bowl on the off side so that he could not be hit. After Sugg had reached his century, W.G. left the field for some refreshment and the acting captain, possibly E.M., immediately put Roberts on and gave him the requested fieldsman on the leg side. Sugg hit the first ball he received straight to the fielder and was rewarded by Roberts with a brandy and soda at the close of the innings.[69] In another match with Gloucestershire, Frank Sugg tells how when his score was above 50 and he was approaching 1,000 runs for the season, a shower of rain left Arthur Mold's footholds half full of water and 'a great trial' to the batsman. With help from his wife, two small boys were persuaded, in return for half a crown apiece, to purchase two sponges at a local chemist's shop which were then stamped into the footholds to absorb some of the moisture. Dr E.M. Grace (whose lob bowling had been plundered by Frank on a number of occasions) saw what was going on, raced out of the pavilion, and bundled the boys off the ground with a minimum of ceremony so Frank 'never reaped the full fruition of his ingenuity.'[70] Although

69 *Sporting Chronicle*, 1 August 1916, and Bearshaw, *op.cit.*, pp 110-111.
70 J.A.H.Catton, *Wickets and Goals*, pp 39-40. Catton reports the story was told to him by Frank Sugg. Frank gave further currency to the story in an interview in *Sporting Chronicle*, 25 July 1916.

the story was often re-told, its provenance has to be in doubt for the facts as described do not fit those of any Gloucestershire home match involving Frank Sugg and Lancashire. Stories can often be improved by embroidery!

Returning to the 1893 season, the most praiseworthy of Sugg's three hundreds was probably the 127 against Nottinghamshire at Trent Bridge. Notts scored 318 in their first innings, Arthur Shrewsbury accounting for 148 of them. Not to be outdone, Lancashire replied with 322, with Sugg, batting at three, making his 127 out of 178 while he was at the wicket. Nottinghamshire were then dismissed for 92, Mold and Briggs sharing the wickets. Lancashire struggled to get the runs needed for victory, losing six wickets for 55, including Sugg without scoring, before Smith and Baker saw them home without further loss. As this pair of scores shows, Sugg had not eradicated his vulnerability early in an innings - he was out for a duck ten times in 1893 - but his heavier run-scoring was rewarded by selection for the North against the Australians and for the Players in both their matches against the Gentlemen. He was, however, out cheaply in all his innings in these matches, just as he had been when Lancashire met the Australians early in the season, and there was no chance of his winning a place in the Test team.[71] (His colleagues, Ward and Mold, did win their first caps in this season, however.) For the first time in Frank Sugg's career, he made more than one thousand runs in all first-class matches, finishing the season with 1,047 runs but his average of 24.92 was well down on that in championship matches alone.

Crosfield was not available for the 1894 season and the captaincy reverted to A.N.Hornby. However Hornby failed to show up for Lancashire's ninth match of the season against Nottinghamshire at Trent Bridge and the 22-year-old Archie MacLaren took over the position thereon. The season had started badly for Lancashire, six of the first seven championship matches being lost, and although results later in the season were better, only seven of the 16 championship matches were won. Lancashire finished joint fourth with Kent behind Surrey, Yorkshire and Middlesex. Once again

71 In the Players' first innings at Lord's, Sugg was dismissed by a 'famous' catch, nonchalantly taken by wicketkeeper Gregor MacGregor, standing up to the stumps. He held it low down to his right off Charles Kortright, bowling at his frenzied fastest. P.F.Warner described Kortright's 'muzzle velocity' as a hundred miles an hour, though he had no means of measuring it. As we now know, perhaps he wasn't far wrong.

Mold and Briggs were outstanding, Mold taking 187 wickets at 11.60 and Briggs 137 at 13.83. Without them, Lancashire's season would have been a sorry one indeed.

Frank Sugg's season also started badly. In his first ten appearances he mustered only 186 runs in 18 innings, an average score of 10.33. There was serious talk of dropping him. Fortunately his form improved and he eventually scored 1,033 runs, the second time he totalled over a thousand runs in a season. His average was 27.18, higher in the first-class list than any other Lancashire player. Sugg appeared in all 16 championship games and scored 717 runs at 28.68, Baker pipping him for first place in the Lancashire championship averages. He made two centuries, both against Somerset, 105 at Old Trafford, the innings that ended his dismal start to the season, and 157 not out at Taunton. In the match at Old Trafford, Somerset batted first and were shot out for 31, Mold taking seven for 10 in nine devastating five-ball overs, including the hat-trick, all clean bowled, with Briggs taking the

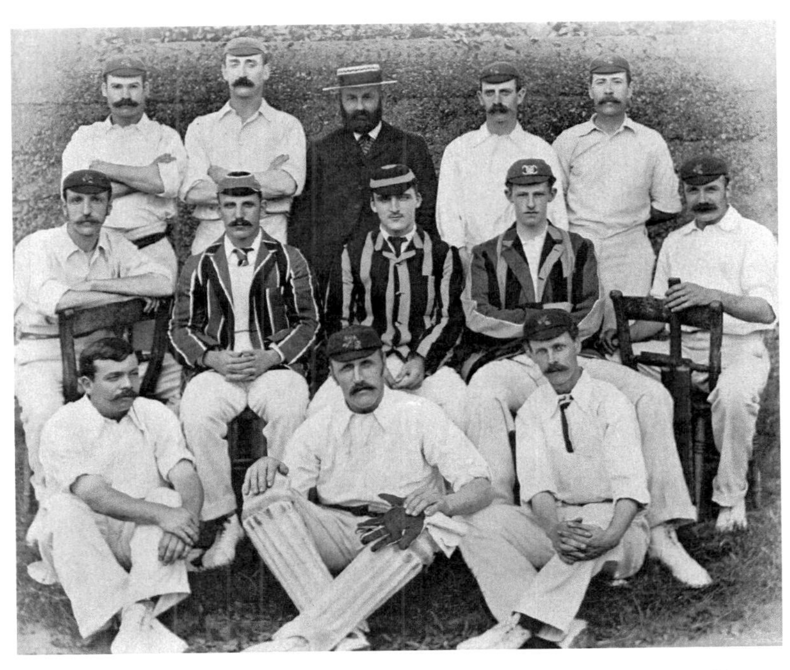

The Lancashire side which finished fourth in the Championship in 1894. Standing (l to r): A.W.Mold, A.G.Paul, S.Lunt (scorer), G.R.Baker, A.P.Smith. Seated: A.Ward, S.M.Tindall, A.C.MacLaren (capt), G.R.Bardswell, F.H.Sugg. On the ground: J.Briggs, C.Smith (wk), A.Tinsley.

other three. For Lancashire, Sugg and Ward put on 131 for the second wicket but wickets fell steadily after that and Lancashire's final total was 231, Sugg having contributed almost half the runs with sustained aggressive batting. Somerset did a little better in their second innings, scoring 132, but leaving Lancashire easy winners by an innings and 68 runs. Mold took six for 50 in that innings, giving him match figures of 13 for 60. The return match with Somerset at Taunton a week later was drawn. Batting first, Lancashire scored 260 for two wickets on the first day, with Sugg 157 not out and having despatched six deliveries into the neighbouring churchyard, when rain prevented any play on the second day. In search of victory, MacLaren declared the innings closed. Somerset were put out for 168, Briggs taking seven for 71 and Mold three for 89, but no further play was possible.

Sugg had the satisfaction in 1894 of adding to his number of wickets in first-class cricket. Against Nottinghamshire in the match in which MacLaren took on the captaincy, Sugg bowled 11 overs of his slows and captured two wickets for 34 runs. His victims were celebrated ones indeed, William Gunn[72] and William Barnes. According to Sugg, 'Barnes said it was impossible to forgive me for such a deed, and he still says so. When he got out he told me that he had come to the conclusion that it was quite time he gave up cricket.'[73] He was joking of course.

The County Championship was increased from nine counties to fourteen in 1895 with the addition of Derbyshire, Essex, Hampshire, Leicestershire and Warwickshire. (Lancashire had included Derbyshire and Leicestershire among their first-class fixtures in the previous season, before they were admitted to the Championship.) Lancashire had an excellent season, finishing second to Surrey in the Championship. The key to their success was the continuing outstanding bowling of Mold and Briggs. Mold had his best-ever season, taking 182 championship wickets for 13.71, and Johnny Briggs was not far behind with 119 wickets at 15.10. The dependence of the side on these two bowlers is illustrated by the fact that the next highest wicket-taker was the newcomer A.W.Hallam with 28 wickets. Another newcomer was J.T.Tyldesley who was to be a leading batsman for the county in the coming seasons.

---

72 Sugg took Gunn's wicket twice in first-class cricket, the only batsman to suffer this indignity.

73 *Cricket*, 26 April 1896.

But if 1895 was to be anyone's season, that accolade has to go to the 23-year-old Archie MacLaren. In the previous winter he had toured Australia with A.E.Stoddart's side and was re-appointed Lancashire's captain for the 1895 season. But he had accepted a teaching post at a Harrow prep school and had to absent himself from the side after a couple of early games. He returned to the side for the match against Somerset at Taunton in July when, opening the innings with Albert Ward, he scored 424, breaking W.G.Grace's record for the highest individual first-class innings, 344 for MCC against Kent in 1876. MacLaren's almost chanceless innings[74] lasted for seven hours and 50 minutes. One of a number of enterprising partnerships in Lancashire's total of 801 was one of 95 runs in 45 minutes with Sugg for the fifth wicket, Sugg scoring 41 in that time. Later in the season MacLaren scored hundreds in three successive innings and he topped the Lancashire averages by a wide margin.

Old Trafford in 1895, with its then new pavilion and, to judge from the batsman's position, perhaps Frank Sugg batting.
He played in 111 first-class matches on this ground.

Sugg played in 21 of his county's 22 championship matches but his was a rather disappointing season. He made some useful scores early on, including 125 against Kent, but after that innings his performances fell away with 43 in the penultimate match of the summer against Middlesex his next highest score. All told, he scored 779 runs at an average of only 22.91, fifth in the Lancashire averages (of those playing at least 10 matches). Rather surprisingly perhaps, he was chosen for the Players against the Gentlemen at Lord's. His performance in this prestigious fixture mirrored that of

74 Though Sugg reported that he was told 'on the highest authority' that S.M.J.Woods' first ball to MacLaren 'distinctly grazed the stumps but not with sufficient force to dislodge the bails.' *Frank Sugg Pocket Cricket Annual*, 1897, p 46.

his season as a whole: he scored 31 in the Players' first innings of 231 but, on a good wicket with the Players on course to a match winning total of 363 in their second innings, Frank holed out in the deep for a duck. *Wisden*'s verdict on Frank Sugg's season was harsh but eloquent: 'Sometimes his cricket was such as to make the judicious grieve.'

Frank Sugg must have had some concerns for his place when the players assembled for the start of the 1896 season. But in terms of runs scored it was to be the most successful of his career. After losing their first championship match, Lancashire won eight matches in succession and seemed odds-on favourites to win the title. However injuries, the most damaging being the hand injury suffered by Mold, and late in the season some bad luck with the weather, spoiled their chances and they finished second to Yorkshire with 11 wins out of their 22 matches. MacLaren was again able to play little part until the end of term at Harrow, the captaincy in his absence devolving to Ernest Rowley or Hornby. Not only because of the injury to Mold, Lancashire's bowling was less penetrative than in the previous season, but their batsmen were much more productive in 1896. MacLaren, who played in only ten championship matches, headed the averages with 54.84 and a highest score of 226 not out. Behind him came Frank Sugg who played in all the county's championship matches, further testimony to his fitness, and scored a total of 1,278 runs at an average of 39.93. Third in the averages was George Baker with 35.69. Frank had three centuries in 1896, the first of which was 110 against Sussex early in the season, 'an innings which was remarkable for all the vigour for which he has made himself famous,'[75] the second 220 against Gloucestershire, and the third 151 against Leicestershire. Sugg almost reached another hundred in a high-scoring match against Derbyshire but fell four runs short.

The double hundred at Bristol, towards the end of June, was to be the highest score of Sugg's career. After Gloucestershire had been dismissed for 133 with Baker taking six for 18 off 22.1 overs (and Mold, through injury, able to bowl only two overs), Lancashire replied with 389. The weather was very hot and the boundaries at the Bristol ground set very deep. Sugg, opening the innings with Albert Ward, hit his 220 runs, which included 35 fours, in only three hours and 40 minutes. In the pre-lunch session on the

75 *Cricket*, 21 May 1896.

second day he took his score from 59 - some reports say 60 - to 204. At the end of his innings, caught by an unidentified substitute, he was completely exhausted, in part perhaps because his innings contained eight threes. Johnny Tyldesley was the next highest scorer with 63. Gloucestershire did not entirely crumble after this onslaught but were all out for 238, W.G.Grace carrying his bat for 102, seven wickets falling to Johnny Briggs, leaving Lancashire the victors by an innings and 18 runs. Although it was his highest score, Sugg's 220 was far from chanceless, even though the red *Lillywhite* annual thought it 'an exceedingly fine display'. Early in his innings he was given not out after a ball grazed his glove and was caught by the wicketkeeper, a decision which had W.G. grumbling and chuntering throughout the match, and he was missed three times during his innings, albeit only one an apparently easy chance. Frank Sugg had no qualms about standing his ground when he knew he was out, taking the pragmatic, if unethical, line: 'Of course a batsman has to take good and bad decisions as all in the day's work. If you get given in when you're out it is as well to remember that sometimes you're given out when you're really in. A sort of rough justice gets done in the end.'[76] In the Golden Age of the amateur cricketer, this might seem a professional's view of how the game should be played, but Sugg could have reflected that W.G. was not pure white when it came to the game's ethics and even as haughty an amateur as Archie MacLaren admitted to not walking when he knew he was out.[77] What view Frank took about the issue of walking when he came to don the umpire's coat himself is another matter.

The Australians were touring England again in 1896. There was little chance of Frank being chosen for the England side but he did encounter the Australians in five matches. Two of these were for Lancashire and three were for invitation sides, C.E. de Trafford's XI, the North (for which fixture no Yorkshire or Derbyshire players were available), and a rather weak Players team at Leyton where he captained a side for the first time in his first-class career. The Australians won all these matches with some ease. Sugg's contributions were modest. His highest score in his ten innings was 25 in Lancashire's first match against the tourists. Frank would have been disappointed by his performances in these matches but he did have the satisfaction in mid-season, straight

76 *Sporting Chronicle*, 1 August 1916.
77 Michael Down, *Archie: a Biography of A.C.MacLaren*, Allen and Unwin, 1981, p 49.

after the Leyton match, of being selected for the Players against the Gentlemen at Lord's and again of captaining the side, recognition of his contribution to the professional game over a considerable number of seasons rather than of his captaincy skills which, it has to be said, were virtually unknown. For all Frank Sugg's reputation as a smiter, however, he had a keen appreciation of the finer points of the game. The two sides that took the field at Lord's were packed with star players of the day, the Gentlemen's first seven batsman being W.G.Grace as captain, A.E.Stoddart, K.S.Ranjitsinhji, L.C.H.Palairet, F.S.Jackson, A.C.MacLaren and Sir T.C.O'Brien, while the Players' main strength was perhaps in their bowling which included Tom Richardson, Johnny Briggs, George Lohmann and J.T.Hearne. The Gentlemen scored 268 in their first innings and then dismissed the Players for only 116, Sugg scoring a creditable 33. Following on, the Players did better, scoring 373, of which Tom Hayward contributed 116 not out and J T Hearne 71. Frank Sugg scored 22, one of five victims of W.G.Grace. The amateurs hit off the 221 required for victory for the loss of only four wickets. Despite the disappointment of the result, the match was a satisfactory one for the Players' captain. But it was to be Frank Sugg's last appearance in the fixture.

In all first-class matches in 1896 Sugg scored 1,439 runs at an average of 31.28. The total was the highest aggregate of his career by a considerable margin. It was in this 1896 season that Sugg first used a new bat manufactured and patented by his firm. It is impossible to say whether this contributed to the success he was to enjoy during the season but *Wisden*, whether aware of the novelty of his bat or not, had no doubt to what to attribute the improvement in Sugg's performance: 'Preserving his exceptional powers as a hitter to the full, he displayed, except on some notable occasions, far more control over himself than has been his custom and he met with his reward.'

Sugg was called upon to bowl a few overs in three consecutive Lancashire matches in August 1896. His 24 overs, all delivered after the regular bowlers had been toiling for a while, yielded four wickets for 77 runs, 40 per cent of the wickets he was to take in first-class cricket. His bowling average of 19.25 put him 'technically' third in Lancashire's list behind Mold and Hallam but above Johnny Briggs. His best figures were two for 40 off 11 overs against Sussex when his victims included the prized wicket of

Ranji, stumped when attempting to hit one of Sugg's slows out of the ground.

Now 34 years old, Frank Sugg could be very pleased with the way his season, his tenth for Lancashire, had gone in 1896. The Lancashire committee recognised his contribution over the preceding decade by awarding Frank a benefit match in the 1897 season. With A.N.Hornby once again taking over the captaincy from MacLaren, Lancashire played 26 matches in the Championship in 1897, four more than in the previous season,[78] and Frank Sugg played in all but two of them. He would no doubt have played in every game had he not suffered a broken finger in the match against Surrey at Kennington Oval when he was hit by one of many fearsome deliveries sent down by Tom Richardson (earlier he had had his bat broken) when there were two further matches to play. With Surrey and Lancashire fighting it out for the Championship, it was a vital match. Surrey won by six wickets but on the scoring system then in place Lancashire went on to snatch the title even though Surrey won 17 matches to Lancashire's 16 and beat their northern opponents in both their matches.

It was in many respects a wonderful season for Lancashire. At last the bowling was less dependent on Mold and Briggs, with the 32-year-old Willis Cuttell, another Yorkshireman, taking over 100 wickets and Albert Hallam 90, the two bringing needed variety to the attack. The bowlers secured 444 wickets at 17.95 runs each, the lowest average of any county in the Championship, in a year in which, overall, wickets cost 22.69 apiece. The batting, worth 25.89 a wicket, remained more than adequate. MacLaren, who once more was available for only a few matches, again headed the batting averages, followed by Ward, Baker, Tyldesley and Frank Sugg. Sugg scored 972 runs in the Championship at an average of 31.35. Adding in his two other first-class matches against MCC and the Gentlemen of Philadelphia, Sugg scored 1,023 runs at 30.08, and it was in this season that he passed the mark of 10,000 runs in first-class cricket. Although he only hit one century, 122 against Yorkshire at Old Trafford late in the season, he had fifties in another eight innings. Against Essex at Leyton, he scored 88 not out and 81, one of the very few instances where Frank got a big score in both innings. Frank regarded his century against Yorkshire the finest innings he ever played. As he explained, 'That

78 The additional fixtures were with Essex and Hampshire.

score was made on three wickets. It was the same pitch of course but it varied between reasonably hard, soft and sticky. No one else on our side reached fifty and when I got to three figures the public were very pleased and the locomotives on the adjoining railway whistled cock-a-doodle-do at least as well as the drivers could make them.'[79]

For his benefit match Sugg chose the visit of Kent to Old Trafford, commencing on 7 June. Hornby, now 50 years old and finally coming to the end of his distinguished career, had promised that he would captain Lancashire and Lord Harris agreed to play for Kent, his first match at Old Trafford for ten years and evidence of the good relationship that Frank Sugg had with the 'high and mighty' of the game. He could look forward to a successful benefit. His big hitting and fast scoring made him a very popular cricketer, and his prowess at other sports added to his appeal. The brothers' flourishing Sugg sports business made Frank's name a familiar one to a wider Lancashire public than those who attended cricket matches. Frank's expectations for his benefit were borne out on the opening day of the match, Whit Monday, when in fine weather a crowd of 21,916 paying spectators plus at least 1,800 members packed into Old Trafford. Kent batted first and were all out for 192, Mold taking four wickets, one of them Lord Harris, bowled for four, and Briggs three wickets. Replying, Lancashire were 103 for four at the close with Tyldesley 49 not out. Frank Sugg had received 'a great ovation' on going out to bat but he scored only eight before he was bowled by Walter Wright, Kent's left-arm fast-medium bowler. (Left-arm quick bowlers often proved Frank's undoing.) Then the rain came and with such a vengeance that no play was possible on the remaining two days. Frank's disappointment would have been leavened by the £830 that was raised for the beneficiary on the first day. The Lancashire committee opened the subscription lists with a donation of £50 and when they were closed the final amount raised for Frank bordered on £1,000. There is little doubt that if the match had gone its full course the sum would have been the largest of any Lancashire player's benefit to that date.[80] The sums of £830 and

79 *Sporting Chronicle*, 1 August 1916.
80 Richard Pilling's benefit in 1889 raised £1,500. By contrast, Walter Sugg's benefit, with a smaller county, Derbyshire in 1898, raised £340. His benefit match, against Yorkshire at Chesterfield in August, was the famous game in which J.T.Brown and John Tunnicliffe put on 554 for the visitors' first wicket.

£1,000 would be equivalent to about £71,000 and £85,500 in 2011 money.

Frank was well aware that many professional cricketers were less fortunate than himself and often faced straightened times, if not penury, when their professional careers came to an end. With his brother Walter, he did what he could to help in cases known to him. For example, John Jackson, the Nottinghamshire allrounder who lived in Liverpool,[81] was 'in no small measure' assisted by the Sugg brothers and after his death in a Liverpool workhouse in 1901 Frank appealed for funds to ensure that his grave would not 'remain unmarked.'[82] The appeal was unsuccessful and it was only in 2009 that a headstone was finally raised on Jackson's grave. The irony of this is that Frank Sugg's final resting place is also unmarked, on which more in the final chapter.

Returning to Frank's time as a stalwart of the Lancashire team, Lancashire failed in 1898 to attain the high standards they had established in winning the Championship the previous season and slipped to sixth place in the table, conceding the title to Yorkshire. It was Lancashire's bowling in particular that let them down and they conceded almost five more runs per wicket than in 1897. Although Cuttell completed the double, the first Lancashire cricketer to do so, Hallam was unable to play at all and Briggs was not the force of old. Mold was again hit by injuries, as was Hallows, an allrounder who otherwise would have been a valuable addition to the bowling resources. Johnny Tyldesley was the county's outstanding batsman. Sugg was less successful than in the previous season. He scored 1,037 runs in his 22 championship matches at an average of 26.58 and 1,044 runs at 25.46 in his 23 first-class matches. He made a terrible start to the season, 'palpably out of form' according to *Wisden*. His scores in his first 11 innings were one, six, six, nought, nought, nought, seven, 12, 28, nought and six, putting his position in the side in doubt. On the county's West Country tour, in June, he recovered his form with 169 against Somerset, when he shared in a third-wicket partnership of 278 in three hours with Albert Ward in Lancashire's second innings,[83] and a spirited 76 against Gloucestershire. He

81 Jackson had been a predecessor of Sugg at Burnley, where he was the club's professional in 1868 and 1869, but had moved to Merseyside in 1870.

82 Old Ebor (A.W.Pullin), *Old England Cricketers*, Wm. Blackwood, 1900, p 56, and Ric Sissons, *op.cit.*, p 147.

83 At the time this was the highest third-wicket partnership for the county, a record overtaken in 1904. At the end of the 2010 season, it was still the county's record for the third-wicket partnership against Somerset.

scored another hundred in 1898, 104 against Essex at Old Trafford, and added 70 in Lancashire's second innings (though Essex ran out comfortable winners by four wickets). But his continuing inconsistency and fallibility early in an innings diminished Frank Sugg's value to his side.

It was in this season that Frank achieved the 'best' bowling figures of his career, two for 12 in 5.2 five-ball overs against Notts at Trent Bridge, one of them William Gunn, in 'a spiritless match' that was fizzling out into a draw.

'Monkey' Hornby, now 52 years old, relinquished the captaincy for the 1899 season, the position being shared between MacLaren and G.R.Bardswell. But Bardswell only played in four championship matches and Alec Eccles and Hornby also had to fill the role in some games. This unsatisfactory situation hardly helped the team's prospects; not surprisingly Lancashire had another disappointing season, finishing fourth behind Surrey, Middlesex and Yorkshire. The bowling suffered from injuries to Hallam and the serious illness suffered by Johnny Briggs during the Test match at Headingley, an illness which ended his season and was to be the beginning of the end of his great career. Arthur Mold, now also nearing the end of his career, took 104 wickets at 19.34, followed by Cuttell with 74 wickets and Briggs with 49. A useful acquisition was Jack Sharp, a fast-medium bowler who, like Frank Sugg earlier in his career, was also a professional footballer and who in due course was to open a sports business in competition with that of Sugg. Sharp was also to prove an excellent batsman. The county's leading batsman, however, was now Tyldesley who scored 1,584 runs in the Championship in 1899 at an average of 41.68 and was selected for England during the season. Towards the end of the 1899 season, the similarly brilliant R.H.Spooner, then just 18 years old, arrived on the scene and played in four matches.

It was during this season that Sugg's position in the side came under serious threat for the first time. He was in the twelve for Lancashire's first match but was left out of the final eleven in favour of C.R.Hartley, a 26-year-old amateur, who had first played for the county two seasons previously. Johnny Tyldesley was moved into Frank Sugg's favoured spot of first wicket down. Sugg was still out of the side when Lancashire were soundly beaten by the Australians, in each Lancashire innings only Tyldesley and Cuttell reaching double figures. He returned to the side against

Leicestershire when Tyldesley was on England duty but was then left out for the next two matches. The writing was beginning to look to be on the wall for Frank. He soon came back once more, doing well against Derbyshire and Somerset, when he scored 95 in an innings of spectacular hitting, missed chances, and a foolishly attempted run which cost him a probable century. He was at the wicket for only one hour and forty five minutes and 64 of his runs came in boundaries.

What was to prove Frank Sugg's last first-class match was against Yorkshire at Bramall Lane, Sheffield, starting on 26 June 1899. Lancashire won by 59 runs. Other than a couple of catches, Sugg did little of note in the match. Indeed, sadly, in his last innings in a first-class match, Frank was out for a duck, caught Tunnicliffe, bowled Rhodes. After this innings he disappeared from the first-class game with nothing to mark his going, in sharp contrast to his explosive performances as batsman and outfielder in earlier summers. In this final season Sugg scored 250 runs at an average of 25.00. *Wisden*, in its comment on Lancashire's season, said that Sugg 'played fairly well at times and considering the big deeds he has accomplished for the county, his abilities as a forcing batsman and his excellence as an outfield, the wisdom of the executive in dropping him so completely seemed open to question.' In reality though, Lancashire now had six or seven players who could reliably take the middle-order batting positions from which he had given such entertainment. Whatever the wisdom of the decision, Frank, now 38 years old, had plenty of other interests with which to fill his time.[84] He would also soon have a growing family to look after.

Before we turn to consider the life that Frank Sugg made for himself after his retirement from first-class cricket, it will be of interest to recount the assessment of him made by W.G.Grace at the end of Frank's career. According to W.G., who had observed Sugg in action at close quarters throughout his career, Sugg was

> a batsman of the dashing order, a tremendous hitter and when he has got his 'eye in' punishes any kind of bowling he may have to face. Batsmen like Sugg are the terror of bowlers who never know to what extent they may be punished. Sugg might have made a better batsman if he had been gifted with a little

84 His brother Walter, eighteen months older, continued to play for Derbyshire, where there was far less competition from other players, until 1902, though not regularly.

> more patience. His hard, clean driving and his splendid hitting to leg are delightful to watch. As long as he is at the wicket he hits with splendid impartiality at good or bad balls and generally gets out caught at the wicket or in the long field. No doubt these hitters are towers of strength to their side and I am much too fond of lively cricket not to appreciate their value. I have seen Sugg keep a crowd in roars of laughter and applause by his tremendous hitting. He is a very strong hitter and when he gets hold of a ball the probabilities of its failing to reach the boundary are remote. The drawback with batsmen like Sugg is that they are never reliable. Nevertheless, more matches are won by hitters than by stonewallers, and when my time comes for watching instead of playing I shall hope that batsmen like Frank Sugg will be plentiful.[85]

To the Doctor, Frank Sugg the batsman was clearly not the complete article. To cricket followers around the country, however, he was a very popular player and his entertainment value more than compensated for any defensive failings.

85 W.G.Grace, *Cricketing Reminiscences and Personal Recollections*, James Bowden, 1899, pp 384-385.

Chapter Nine
Away From Old Trafford

The most fascinating aspect of the life of Frank Sugg is the way he combined his thirteen seasons with Lancashire as a professional cricketer with the founding and development, with his brother Walter, of a successful sports business. The interconnection of his two interests is nicely illustrated by Frank's remark that he took up golf in order to be better able to procure and sell golf equipment and clothing in his shops (and, typically of the man, he made himself into an excellent golfer). The next chapter of this book will give a detailed account of the sports business from its inception in 1888 to its rather messy demise in the late 1920s. In this chapter we will deal with a number of other aspects of Frank Sugg's life after he retired from first-class cricket at the end of the 1899 season up to the end of his business career, sketching in an account of his involvement in sports other than cricket and football.

Of course, Frank did not completely pack away his cricket gear after his final first-class game, for Lancashire against Yorkshire at Bramall Lane, Sheffield, the town in which he learned the rudiments of the game. From his young days through his years in first-class cricket, Frank Sugg had enjoyed club cricket and had played as much of it as his commitments would allow. After his spell with Burnley and during his years with Lancashire, Frank appeared for the Blackburn, Wavertree, Birkdale, Southport and East Lancashire cricket clubs among others, often as a 'match professional'. It was in this capacity that a Blackburn resident, reminiscing about his boyhood in the town, records that he saw Frank Sugg, then first-wicket down for Lancashire, give 'many fine exhibitions' for Blackburn on the town's Alexandra Meadows ground.[86] Frank also played several times for the prestigious Liverpool and District side between 1893 and 1897, including the

86 Charles H.Stirrup, Blackburn When I Was A Boy, *Blackburn Times*, 28 July 1933.

match in 1893 against the touring Australians.[87] During his final season with Lancashire, Frank was apparently approached by W.G.Grace's London County club, but if an offer was made he did not take it up: perhaps the distance from Liverpool and his business commitments ruled out such a venture.

After finishing with the first-class game, Frank played regularly for Birkdale until 1904 - the club amalgamated with Southport in 1902.[88] He scored four centuries for the club, 112 against Birkenhead Victoria in 1901, 102 not out against Bootle in 1902, 101 against Wallasey in 1903 and 108 not out against Neston in 1904, in which season he was the club's vice-captain and Walter the club captain. Frank and his brother Walter played a prominent part in the club's affairs in these years; for example they persuaded the young Derbyshire fast bowler Arnold Warren to become Birkdale's professional in 1901 - Warren was to play in one Test, in 1905 - and they arranged for a Derbyshire XI to visit the club in 1903.[89] Later Frank played for various other local club sides. To give just a few examples, in 1905 he scored 161 for Bootle against Huyton out of a score of 258 for eight with the next highest score 35; in 1908 he toured Ireland with Birkenhead Victoria and scored 406 in six innings, including 107 against Phoenix; in 1910 he toured Ireland again, this time with Birkenhead Park and scored 215 not out against Pembroke and 105 against County Wicklow; in the same season, back home, he scored 79 not out for Bootle against Birkenhead Park; also in 1910 he played again for Wavertree, the club history commenting 'whilst he was in his late forties, he must have been a great asset to the club' but giving no scores.[90] As this comment suggests, Frank Sugg's reputation for big hitting and fast scoring made him a big draw in any of the matches in which he appeared after retiring from the first-class scene.

Frank was not a stranger to Ireland when he joined the tours in 1908 and 1910. While still at Lancashire, he had been engaged as professional and coach at Clongowes Wood College, a boarding school for boys near Clane in County Kildare and one of the oldest Catholic schools in the country. Frank, who was not a Catholic

87 Don Ambrose, *Liverpool and District Cricketers: 1882-1947,* ACS Publications, 2002.
88 The club's ground is one of Lancashire CCC's present 'outgrounds'.
89 I am grateful to Michael Braham of the Birkdale-Southport club for the information on Frank Sugg's time with the club.
90 *151 Years: History of Wavertree CC*, 2006, p 29.

himself (he was a Christian Scientist), had probably responded to a newspaper advertisement of the post. There was a twice-daily ferry service from Liverpool to Dublin at the time Frank took up his appointment in 1893 (though the crossing took eight hours) so the school was relatively accessible to him. In 1893 the school had a fixture list of half a dozen or so matches and the standard of its cricket was not very high. Frank had very clear views on what was needed to succeed at the game and he applied himself to his duties diligently. He clearly enjoyed the role of coach and mentor to the boys. Each season Frank played in some of the school's matches, no doubt enjoying himself and not taking the occasions very seriously; in one match against Phoenix Cricket Club in which he scored 54 not out, he is recorded as making 'a sensational hit for 7', no explanation offered.[91] Frank also helped with athletics at the school and officiated at the annual athletics sports day. He

Clongowes Wood College cricket eleven in 1897.
Back row (l to r): F.H.Sugg, H.Flinn, J.Anderson, J.McKenna, W.McCormack.
Middle row: J.Kelly, T.Kyne, F.W.Christian (capt), D.Sherlock, O.J.S.Gogarty.
On the ground: M.Spain, T.Flinn.
None of Sugg's charges pictured here achieved cricketing prominence; Gogarty, though, became a considerable literary figure in Dublin and later a senator in the Irish parliament.

91 *The Clongownian*, 1901, p 39. I am most grateful to Margaret Doyle, archivist at Clongowes Wood College, for extracting references to cricket and Frank Sugg in the school magazine for me.

retained his position at the school for ten years and when he left in 1904 (to be succeeded by John Gunn of Nottinghamshire), his contribution to cricket at the school was warmly recognised.[92] The local newspaper commented: 'He was quite the most popular and painstaking coach who ever entered this famous seat of sport and learning.'[93] In 1897, past and present members of the school had shown their appreciation by subscribing £19 9s 6d to Frank's benefit fund, a sum which was described in the school magazine as 'substantial' - as indeed it was at the time and in the context.

As far as is known, Frank did not take on any other regular coaching responsibilities after his retirement from first-class cricket. His family believe that at some time he coached at Clifton College, Bristol, but the school archivist has told me that there is no record of Frank ever being a designated professional at the school. He was not able to say whether Frank was an additional coach at Clifton at any time, though, with Frank's Gloucestershire connections, that is a possibility.

It is of course quite usual for cricketers who have played at the top level to extend their playing careers at club level, in some cases as a club professional or coach. What is unusual in Frank Sugg's case is the wider contribution he made to cricket after his first-class career was over. Prominent among these is his founding in 1910 in Liverpool of the Sugg Cricket League. The aim of this sponsorship, as we would now call it, was to encourage the game at the grass-roots level by providing a well-organised and competitive cricket league. Frank was the first president of the League and his commitment ensured the support of other sporting notables in the town. Among the teams participating in the Sugg League was a team made up of employees of the Sugg business. It is possible that Frank turned out at least occasionally for the Sugg team to give a boost to its chances and publicity for the league. In 1911, following Frank's initiative, Walter Sugg established the Sugg Thursday Cricket Club in Sheffield and the following year a Sugg Thursday League was formed with the same purposes as the Liverpool League but designed for teams that could play on

92 James Joyce was a pupil at Clongowes between 1888 and 1892. His time at the school did not overlap with that of Frank Sugg, but with Sugg's distinctive surname one might have expected his inclusion in the passage in *Finnegan's Wake* in which Joyce mentions no fewer than 31 cricket personalities, or in other Joyce works, but Sugg is conspicuous by its absence: see Geoffrey K. Whitelock, Cricket in the Writings of James Joyce, *Journal of the Cricket Society*, Vol.7, No.2, 1975, p 7.

93 Lorna Brown cutting.

Thursday, half-day closing for shops in Sheffield. It is believed that the League was the first midweek league in Yorkshire. Walter Sugg was its first president and Frank Sugg a committee member.

The Sugg Leagues proved very popular and in their heyday attracted enough teams to require a league of several divisions, five in the case of the Sheffield League, including a Saturday section. In the Sheffield League, matches commenced at 3.30 pm and consisted of 40 overs per side with a thirty-minute interval. They were keenly contested. A number of first-class cricketers played in the Sugg Leagues in their early days, the most notable being Fred Trueman who played for Maltby in the Saturday section of the Sugg Thursday League. The league was well enough regarded for top players such as Wilfred Rhodes, Herbert Sutcliffe and Norman Yardley to accept invitations to the Sugg Club and League's annual dinners in Sheffield. It was not until the 1980s that interest began to wane with fewer cricketers able to play on Thursday afternoons and with falling membership of local cricket clubs generally in the face of the widening range of leisure and other attractions available to young people. The Sugg Thursday Cricket Club and League was finally disbanded in 1989, its last president being Timothy Sugg, the third generation of the family after Walter Sugg to hold the post. At the final dinner of the Club, the Suggs' contribution was handsomely recognised: 'We must pay tribute to the Sugg family who have played such a great role in not only the Club but the League bearing their name. Their generosity and support over the years (often unsung and known only to a few) helped both the Club and the League to survive many a crisis.' There were no succeeding generations to take on Frank's mantle in Liverpool and when the end came to the Sugg Cricket League in that city there were, as far as is known, none of the eulogies expressed in Sheffield. Nevertheless, Frank Sugg could be very proud of the contribution he had made to the furtherance of cricket in Liverpool as well as in Sheffield.

It might be far-fetched to say that the Sugg brothers had a mission to promote the game of cricket among the young for there was certainly a commercial side to their commitment to the Sugg cricket leagues; no doubt it encouraged many clubs and individual members to purchase equipment from Sugg shops. The league helped to make Sugg a household name in each of the towns. Similar motives lay behind one of the more interesting Sugg joint ventures, the *Frank Sugg Pocket Cricket Annual.*

Before the advent of radio and television, which were the seed-corn for the growth of present-day mass communications, the British public, or at least the portion of it that could read, had to rely on the printed word for news and information about sport. At the time that Frank Sugg was making his way in the world of sport, there was a great demand to be satisfied as participation and interest in sport among the population increased. In cricket, national, regional and local newspapers all catered for this demand, the reporting of matches being remarkably detailed by today's standards.

Then there were periodicals devoted to sport, some exclusively to cricket, which covered their subjects in more depth than the newspapers and reported more extensively on sport overseas or in the schools - the public schools at any rate. Examples were the *Sporting Chronicle*, *Athletic News* and *Cricket*. These periodicals would add such inside stories, information and speculation about clubs and players as they could, though compared with the more sensational gossip-type columns of today, these contributions were models of restraint. They often included interviews with, or profiles on, leading players and as we have noted in these pages Frank Sugg was a subject in *Cricket* and in the *Sporting Chronicle*. Finally, there were cricket annuals that reviewed a particular season and included fixtures, records and other statistical information. Some were published by newspapers, others privately - often by sports outfitters - the pre-eminent example being of course the *Wisden* almanack. Others included *James Lillywhite's Cricketers' Annual* (red 'Lilly') and *Frank Sugg's Pocket Cricket Annual.*[94]

This last annual was edited and published by Frank and his brother Walter but seems always to have been known as the Frank Sugg Annual, another example of the higher profile of the younger brother in the cricket world. The annual first appeared in 1894, when both were engaged in first-class cricket, and continued annually until 1905. Copies of the annual are now rare. The 1897 edition is typical. It consists of 200 pages, including photographs and advertisements, some for the Frank Sugg business. As well as potted biographies, the laws of cricket, results and averages for all the counties for the previous season, and cricket records, a distinctive feature of the annual was sections on Advice on Batting,

94 The name of the publication varied slightly from time to time.

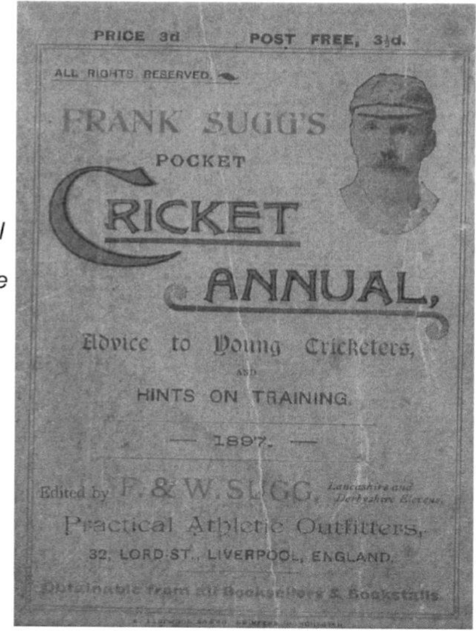

A rarity.

The Frank Sugg annual of 1897, 200 pages of facts and figures, advice and advertisement.

Bowling and Fielding, Advice to Young Cricketers, Hints on Training and the like in which the editors drew explicitly on their own experience. The comprehensive advice on batting, bowling and fielding reads as pertinently today as when it was written with just the occasional dated offering, for example on fielding: 'the pipe and cigarette are in great measure answerable for the many butter fingers that are always *en evidence* wherever cricket is played. Instead of fielding properly, the fragrant weed is lit.' The training regime that Frank recommended for athletes would not go down well today, certainly with present-day cricketers, but it shows the thought that Frank Sugg gave to the matter. Briefly summarised:

Rise early, if possible take a cold bath; "cleanse" the bowels
Take a brisk walk or, if the weather is poor, work out with weights
Breakfast on a chop or steak, toast and a cup of tea
Walk two or three miles followed by a "sharp run" for a mile followed by a vigorous rub down
Dinner at one o'clock of beef or mutton with a glass of beer or stout, greens and potatoes "partaken of sparingly", and a plain wholesome pudding
Rest after dinner, and then a run "in racing costume" of the

distance for which the athlete is preparing
Tea at five or six o'clock, bread and butter, lettuce or watercress, and a couple of new-laid eggs
A quiet walk in the evening to "while away the time until bedtime"
A good night's sound sleep.

Frank's recommendations to youngsters for a healthy life, recommendations which there is every reason to believe he himself followed, would be enthusiastically endorsed by today's life-style gurus:

Don't smoke
Don't drink
Don't chew
Get all the sleep you can
Get all the pure fresh air you can
Eat plain wholesome food and plenty of it.

The annual's small format, the photographs and the low price, 3d (1.25 pence in decimal money), suggest that the *Annual* was aimed at a larger, and perhaps less erudite, audience than *Wisden*. There is no suggestion that the brothers contracted out production of the *Annual*. It has the hallmark of their own work, for example, in the cricket anecdotes feature, which draws on Frank's fund of tales, and the references to matches in which he played in the sections on advice to young cricketers. The anecdotes were intended to entertain by adding colourful detail about players and incidents in matches that would escape the notice of a newspaper reporter in the pressbox, though anecdotes of unusual dismissals or interpretations of the Laws could be instructive as well as amusing. From the several pages of anecdotes (or 'Odds and Ends' as they were titled in some issues), I will restrict myself to this one (abbreviated) example from the 1897 issue: in a Derbyshire v Essex match, Walter Sugg was chasing a hit towards a long boundary. Earlier in the match he had damaged his arm. Seeing that the batsmen had already run four, and fearing that they could run one or two more with his weak throw-in, Walter kicked the ball over the boundary rope. The umpire signalled a boundary but the batsmen argued for four runs for the hit and four for overthrows. Frank adds that the umpires wrote to MCC for guidance should something similar occur in the future 'but their answer did not transpire'.

The annual was printed by a local jobbing printer and was distributed through newsagents and railway kiosks as well as by post (when the cost was 3½d). Whether, after paying royalties, licence fees for including the laws of the game and the first-class averages, and fees to guest contributors, for example, the *Annual* made a trading profit cannot be established but, even if it did not, the advertising medium that the annual provided and the publicity it generated among the cricket-following public must have been a justification for its publication. However, competition from the increasingly diverse print media finally overwhelmed the *Annual* and it ceased publication after the 1905 edition. Although it has now been largely forgotten, today's cricket followers will find the *Frank Sugg Pocket Cricket Annual* an interesting and nostalgic read.

The brothers also published a companion football annual with a similar purpose and a similar format and style. These annuals provided Frank with valuable commercial experience which was useful for his sports business, and developed his writing and editing expertise which he was able to make use of some years later when he tried his hand at journalism for the local paper in Liverpool.

There are other examples of Frank Sugg's mission to increase interest and participation in sport. He was a vice-president of the Leeds League, founded in 1928 and later the West Yorkshire Association Football League, with the aim of bringing all open-age teams in the Leeds area under one organisation.[95] Frank had no obvious connections with football in Leeds, but his name counted for enough for the League to want him in this honorary position. More interestingly, Frank gave his support to the effort in the 1920s to establish a Ladies' Football Association with the object of promoting football as a game that could be enjoyed by women as well as by men. The Football Association strongly opposed the campaign. Frank had no time for those who argued that playing football would be damaging to a girl's health and femininity. Throughout his life, and in his publications, he propagated the view that sport and exercise were as essential to a healthy life for girls and women as they were for boys and men. Lancashire was one of the strongholds of women's football and Frank did what he could at the local level to improve the standard of the women's

95 See www.Kirklees.gov.uk/community/localorgs

game, including by forming his own club, the Mersey Amazons – perhaps not the most apt of names.[96]

Among the sports at which Frank Sugg excelled was the unusual one – for a cricketer anyway – of long-distance swimming. Public swimming baths were among the municipal buildings that were built in Victorian Britain by the councils of the larger towns to provide educational and recreational opportunities for their citizens. The first municipal swimming bath in Sheffield was opened in 1869 and several more were added before the end of the century. It must have been in one of these that Frank learned to swim as a youngster and it would be in character for him to have participated in the swimming competitions that were regularly organised by local swimming clubs. But it was after the Sugg brothers moved to Liverpool that Frank became seriously involved in the sport, his strength and stamina being well suited to the longer-distance events. He took part in long-distance swims on Lake Windermere and in Morecambe Bay, almost certainly uniquely among professional cricketers.

References to Frank Sugg in the cricket literature invariably mention long-distance swimming as one of his sports and his association with Ted Heaton and Thomas Burgess who were among the best-known Channel swimmers in Frank's time. The obituary of Frank in *Wisden,* for example, says 'Sugg joined with Burgess and Heaton in swims.'

Frank befriended Ted Heaton who was superintendent of Liverpool Corporation baths and a well-known character in the town where he was known as 'Professor of Swimming'. Heaton was a leading light in long-distance swimming events such as at Morecambe Bay and Lake Windermere and he made seven attempts to swim the English Channel between 1905 and 1911. None of these was successful. Thomas Burgess was a Yorkshireman who lived in Paris, but was also known to Sugg through his association with Ted Heaton. Burgess made no fewer than 23 attempts to swim the Channel between 1904 and 1922, succeeding only once, in 1911. This was the first successful attempt after Captain Webb's pioneering swim 36 years

96 Patrick Brennans, 'The English Ladies' Football Association', at www.donmouth.co.uk. Sugg's team was entered in the first round of the Ladies' Football Association's first Challenge Cup competition but the Amazons' match against Rochdale never took place, perhaps because of local opposition. The team may have been short-lived.

previously. Burgess and Heaton also made one joint attempt, intended as an experiment in mutual support, but the ebb tide proved too strong and the attempt had to be abandoned.

Cross-Channel swimming was a keenly competitive business at the time with a prize of £1,000 for any successful swimmer. While this was a very large amount of money, attempts cost a considerable sum, including the cost of hiring the accompanying vessel(s) and the officials who would monitor the swimmer's progress. It was the practice for the main contenders to set up camp at Dover and make an attempt every couple of days or so, depending on the weather and the tides, adding further to the expense.

Frank was a powerful swimmer but there is no suggestion that he ever contemplated the ultimate test of swimming across the English Channel himself. His role was that of a back-up supporter. The comprehensive records of cross-Channel attempts maintained by the Dover Museum do not include the names of persons accompanying the swimmers, but one can find the names of some of the persons in boats accompanying the swimmers in some newspaper reports. For example, the *Folkestone Chronicle* issue of 29 July 1905 reports that 'the Lancashire cricketer, Mr Frank Sugg' was one of the party in the tug *Guisno* of London that accompanied Thomas Burgess on his unsuccessful attempt the previous day and that Ted Heaton was also in the accompanying party. Given Frank Sugg's friendship with Ted Heaton in particular, it must be very likely that he accompanied one or other of Heaton and Burgess on other attempts. These were in no way joy-rides and Frank's willingness to assist Channel swimmers in this way testifies to the keenness of his interest in the sport.[97]

If long-distance swimming is among the more physically demanding of all sports, at the opposite end of the spectrum, so to speak, are the more gentle pursuits of bowls, billiards and rifle shooting. These sports were extremely popular in Victorian England as demonstrated by the considerable coverage they were given in the local newspapers. Frank enjoyed, and attained a good standard, in all three of them. They demand a high degree of eye and hand co-ordination and considerable powers of concentration – one aptitude which Frank did not always display at the crease in cricket.

97 I am grateful to the Dover Museum for the information on cross-Channel swim attempts.

Bowls was a relaxation for many cricketers and bowling greens were often incorporated into cricket grounds.[98] There are two versions of the game, lawn (flat) green bowls and crown green bowls, the latter being played mainly in the north. In Sugg's time, as now, crown green bowling was particularly strong in the north-west. (Blackpool hosted the two classic crown green events, the Talbot Handicap and the Waterloo Handicap.) With either code, competitions between local clubs were keenly fought. But bowls was - indeed is - a very clubbable activity. Sports clubs would invariably have a bowling green and greens were also to be found at many pubs. Frank would have participated in competitions organised among local bowls clubs. Each bowls green, particularly each crown green, has its own characteristics, as does each cricket pitch, and Frank would have enjoyed the challenge that that presented as well as the competition of the game itself. He carried off numerous trophies in the course of many years of playing bowls, though without reaching national prominence.

Another clubbable activity in Frank Sugg's time was billiards. Although the game has a long history, it was not until the nineteenth century that billiards grew in popularity among the population at large. The impetus was the development of methods of manufacturing smooth balls and smooth billiard tables with sprung cushions. (It was not until 1893 that the dimensions of a billiard table were standardised.) Interest in the game then exploded. The game was enjoyed by men of all classes of society: it was unheard of for women to play billiards. No country house would be without a billiards room to which the gentlemen could retire after a good dinner, while for the working man a game of billiards (or later snooker) and a few drinks at the local pub or social club was welcome relaxation after the rigours of the working day. In between, were gentlemen's clubs and sports and social clubs with a more middle-class membership which invariably, in Victorian times, had a billiard table if not a designated billiard room. Many cricketers enjoyed the sport. A glance at any issue of *Wisden* in the 1890s will reveal a number of advertisements for billiard tables. Frank probably first became interested in billiards after his move to Liverpool and his absorption into the clubs of the town. Billiards competitions were organised by the major clubs and billiards associations. Walter Sugg was an outstanding

98 W.G.Grace was elected the first president of the English Bowling Association, the body responsible for flat green bowls, in 1903.

billiards player and it is likely that Frank's enthusiasm for the game was sparked by his brother's successes. At any rate, Frank became a serious enough billiards player himself to win prizes in amateur competitions in the Liverpool area.

Rifle shooting was more of a minority sport than bowls and billiards for the obvious reason that the facilities and equipment were less widely available. But for a well-known sportsman and successful businessman like Frank Sugg an entrée to the sport was easy. He proved to be a more than competent shot, regularly carrying off prizes at local events.

One of Frank Sugg's interests not mentioned in the cricket literature was horse racing. With the continuing success of their sports business in the years around the turn of the nineteenth century, Frank and Walter Sugg were relatively rich men, and they were beginning to enjoy a lifestyle beyond the reach of most professional cricketers. They had many friends among the upper reaches of society in the Liverpool area through their business connections and the many contacts they had made in cricket and other sporting circles. These friends included racehorse owners and racegoers. The Suggs became regular spectators at race meetings at Aintree, Haydock and other local racecourses. In due course, and no doubt with encouragement from friends among the racing fraternity, the brothers decided to invest in racehorses of their own. For a time, around the turn of the century, horse racing became one of the main interests of the Sugg brothers. During 1901, for example, the brothers owned, jointly or singly, six racehorses. They entered these horses in races at various meetings at courses up and down the country, some flat races, some hurdles, and on two occasions a horse owned by Walter Sugg came in first. Frank had no winners in 1901.[99] Only detailed research in the Racing Calendars held by the National Horseracing Museum at Newmarket would establish Frank Sugg's record as an owner in its entirety, but it seems that the horses he owned could not have given Frank much of a return on his investment. While this was a disappointment to him, some compensation was the enjoyment he had from the glamour and excitement of race meetings, and the social occasions that they provided.

99 I am grateful to Alan Grundy of the National Horseracing Museum at Newmarket for researching its archives for information on the Suggs' involvement in horse racing in 1901.

For many, betting is one of the pleasures associated with racegoing. As noted in an earlier chapter, Walter Sugg's descendants believe that in Frank's case the pleasure grew into an addiction and that during the rest of his life Frank ran up some large gambling debts. If Frank Sugg did have a weakness for gambling he would not be alone in that among professional sportsmen, but I must emphasise I have seen no direct evidence that would corroborate the suspicion.

Chapter Ten
Frank's Business Career

In the burgeoning laissez-faire economy of late Victorian England, it was easy to set up in business, especially in retailing. The explosion of interest and participation in organised sports such as cricket, football, tennis and hockey, and the increase in leisure time in which to enjoy such pursuits as cycling, rambling and angling offered ample opportunities to a retailer of sports equipment and clothing. Not surprisingly, in the 1880s and 1890s it became common for well-known sportsmen to use their reputations to found a sports business. In cricket, Richard Daft, William Gunn, Arthur Shrewsbury and Alfred Shaw were notable examples. Frank Sugg was one of a number of Lancashire professionals to go into the retail business at this time. Others included Alec Watson and Johnny Briggs, in partnership with Richard Pilling and then with his widow, in Manchester; Albert Ward in Bolton; George Baker in Bury; and Dickie Barlow in Blackpool.[100]

Frank Sugg in 1896, established in his business career, almost looking the part.

Frank Sugg established his sports goods and outfitter business in 1888 in Liverpool in partnership with his brother Walter, initially at 27 Whitechapel. According to Walter,[101] it was A.G.Steel who suggested the venture to the brothers during a match against H.B.Steel's XI at Birkdale, near Southport, the brothers both being members of Birkdale Cricket Club at the time. A second Liverpool branch of the business soon followed at 32 Lord Street, more impressive premises than the Suggs' original shop. In its early days the business was an unincorporated

100 Ric Sissons, *op.cit.*, p 142.
101 *Cricket*, 23 April 1896.

partnership trading as Frank Sugg, suggesting that Frank was the main force behind the business. His name would have carried more commercial weight than that of his brother, particularly in the Liverpool area. An early advertisement in the cricketing press is one in the 1897 *Wisden* which is headed 'Frank Sugg is well known as a determined batsman. He is desirous of being equally well known for his determination in business to sell Sound Goods (not rubbish) at prices which other firms cannot approach.' He is also described as 'the reasonable practical man'. Featured in the advertisement are cricket bats, balls, leg guards, stumping gloves and cricket bags. Frank Sugg advertisements appeared regularly in *Wisden* and cricket periodicals, in a variety of styles. From 1894, he also made extensive use of his *Pocket Cricket Annual* as an advertising medium. Indeed, while the Annual included among its features advice to young cricketers and hints on training as well as articles, fixtures and cricket records, the publication has to be seen primarily as a means of promoting the name of Frank Sugg and his sports business to the general public; the *Frank Sugg Football Annual* served a similar purpose directed at a different market. Sugg's advertisements often emphasised Frank's personal supervision of the business. Unlike some sportsmen, Frank Sugg was no absentee owner. His business was to be a large part of his life for more than thirty years.

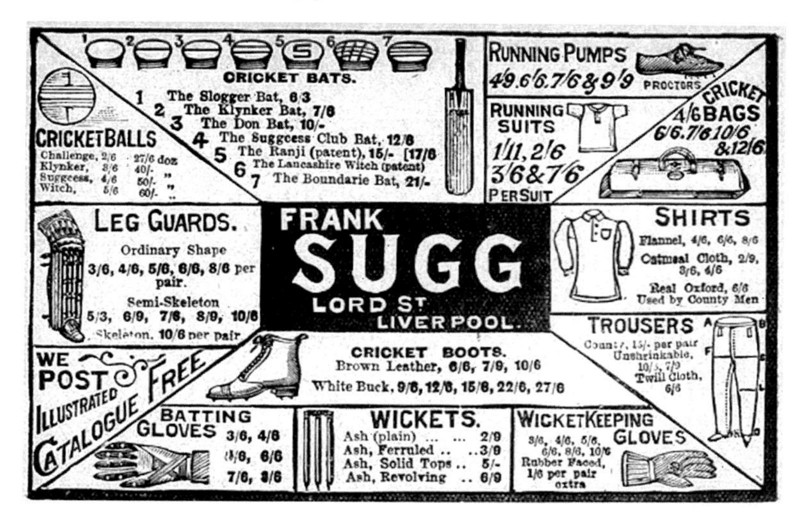

The hard sell.
A Frank Sugg advertisement of 1903.

The market in which he was engaged was highly competitive, with many retailers and their suppliers jockeying for business, as evidenced by the pages of advertisements of sports goods manufacturers and retailers in cricket publications and the keen prices that they featured. The brothers had an eye for other ways of promoting the business than conventional advertising. One was to post the latest cricket scores in the shop window in the expectation that some at least of the watchers would be attracted into the shop. On occasions, the crowd on the pavement was so large that the police intervened and called a halt to the display of the scores. Frank would have noted with some satisfaction that this led to more publicity in the local press.

While some businesses inevitably soon fell by the wayside, the Frank Sugg business prospered and expanded. In 1906, when it claimed to be one of the largest concerns in the industry and had the backing of the Lancashire and Yorkshire Bank, the business was incorporated as Frank Sugg Ltd. Its head office was now at 12 Lord Street, Liverpool, a prestigious shopping street in the centre of the city.[102] It had other branches in Cardiff and Leeds, and manufacturing facilities in Liverpool, in premises adjoining its head office that it had shrewdly acquired, and in Castleford. A branch in Sheffield soon followed. As well as conventional retailing, the firm developed a thriving mail-order business, making use of the excellent railway and postal services of the time.

A letterhead from the early 1900s describes the business as 'manufacturers of cricket, football, hockey, tennis, golf, croquet, fishing tackle and gymnasia', though many of Sugg's products, particularly clothing, would have been bought-in from other, mainly local, manufacturers. The Sugg brothers were not afraid to venture into new lines. For example, the firm began to produce model yachts for such retailers as Gamage's (who were also leading retailers of sports equipment). Model yacht sailing in public parks was a popular family pastime in Edwardian England. Sugg's range of model boats included some of high quality which, to this day, are sought after by collectors.[103] Sugg's also produced horse-riding tackle and clothing, perhaps reflecting the brothers' active involvement in horse racing around the time of this

102 Most of the street's fine buildings were destroyed by enemy bombing in the Second World War.

103 See http://www.vmg.uk/pages/resources/small_boat/sugg.html. Collectable Sugg- branded lawn- and table-tennis equipment, from before 1914, was also advertised on the internet at the end of 2010.

Later Frank Sugg advertisements had artistic qualities.

letterhead. But notwithstanding its diversification, cricket bats and equipment remained the mainstay of the Sugg business. The firm had its own stand of willow trees for bat manufacture. As with other bat makers, production was small-scale and labour-intensive, a skilled craft rather than an industrial activity.

The Sugg brothers were joint managing directors: one of the other two directors, and the company chairman, was Gilbert Jessop. The shareholders' register gives Jessop's occupation as 'gentleman' but he was not a wealthy man and would have had few reservations about becoming a business associate of the Sugg professionals.[104] Jessop was one of the most popular cricketers of his time, with, like Frank Sugg, a talent for big hitting and fast scoring. Frank Sugg had the instinct to appreciate how valuable would be an association with 'The Croucher' from a marketing point of view. Certainly the firm made good use of the association. Illustrative of that is a poster advertisement of Frank Sugg Ltd of Lord Street, Liverpool, featuring Boundarie, Jessop and Invinsa cricket bats. Sugg products were distributed liberally to leading cricketers in return for endorsements. An advertisement for Frank Sugg Ltd in *Athletic News* in 1906 headlines 'Jessop and Fry, a Great Combination who have sent Frank Sugg a Testimonial for the "Boundarie Bat."' (No concern there about conflict of interest for Jessop.) Bat manufacturers vied with each other to incorporate improvements into their bats; many, including Sugg, took out patents, or at least applied for patents, for their innovations. Most involved improvements to handle design, as in the case of Frank Sugg's bat patented in 1896, but some were oddities, for example bat blades that were triangular in cross section or blades that were coated in cork.

After incorporation, the Sugg business continued to expand and more branches were opened. The firm's catalogues, describing the products on offer with their prices, were substantial publications. The 1909 edition of the cricket catalogue, for example, runs to fifty profusely illustrated pages with details of such equipment as lawn mowers, line markers and nets as well as bats, balls, leg guards, gloves, blazers, caps and other cricket paraphernalia, and includes endorsements from several of the leading cricketers of the day,

104 There is no mention of his connection with the Suggs' business in Jessop's autobiography, *A Cricketer's Log*, or in Gerald Brodribb's thoroughly researched book about him, *The Croucher*, published in 1985. This suggests that Jessop's time commitment to the business was limited and that his role was 'non-executive'.

The 'Lancashire Witch' was one of Sugg's better-known patented bats, retailing here at the 2011 equivalent of £50.

including Ranji, Archie MacLaren and the Australians M.A.Noble and W.W.Armstrong.

In 1912, the founding brothers decided the business had reached a stage where conversion into a public limited liability company would be desirable. This led to a disagreement within the family. Frank's son, Frank Reginald, and Walter's son, Hubert Henri Bell (known as Bert) were shareholders in the business. Bert, a man remembered in the family for his trenchant views, disagreed with the proposal and the outcome was that he bought the Sheffield, Nottingham and Hull branches from Frank Sugg Ltd and started a business of his own as HHB Sugg Ltd, a private company incorporated on 3 March 1913 and trading as Sugg Sports, with the Sheffield Snig Hill branch as its headquarters. Frank Sugg Ltd contributed £15,000 by taking up debentures in the new business but the suspicion is that relations between the two businesses, both trading under the Sugg name, were less than warm.

The decision to hive off part of the Frank Sugg Ltd business, and the outbreak of the First World War with a consequent slackening of trade in the sports goods business, meant that any thoughts of conversion into a public company were put on ice. A public-spirited and patriotic man, Frank, aged 52 when the war started, volunteered for military service during which he assisted in the running of prisoner-of-war camps in the Liverpool area. Gilbert Jessop gave up the chairmanship during the war while

In uniform.
Sugg helped run prison camps in the Great War.

continuing as a shareholder, and there were various other changes to the directors of the company aimed at strengthening its capacity for growth in the post-war years. With peace, the economy boomed and business in the sports trade picked up. In 1920 the Sugg business had six UK branches, including one in Holborn, London, the base of its mail-order business, and, in an attempt to increase trade with the Continent, branches in Rotterdam and Antwerp. This renewal of expansion convinced the directors that an injection of additional capital was desirable. In May 1920 the decision was taken to increase the company's nominal capital from £25,000 to £50,000 and to issue 10,000 shares to the public. It was to prove a turning point in the fortunes of Frank Sugg and his company.

The Frank Sugg Ltd premises in Avenue Keyser, Antwerp, shortly before the Great War.

Except for two years during the war, the company had made a profit every year since 1906. In the latest year, the company had made a profit of £4,107 5s 0d on sales of £68,138 0s 4d. Looking forward, the prospectus stated: 'The future prospects of the Athletic Trade have never been so bright as at the present time and it is the aim of the Directors to be in the Forefront of Providers for all classes of Athletic Requisites.' There was no mention of the sale of branches to HHB Sugg Ltd, now a rival in the market.

The issue flopped. Only 665 shares had been allotted by 17 September 1920, with dribs and drabs of further allotments in succeeding weeks. The timing of the issue was unfortunate. The collapse of the boom that followed the war badly hit companies like Frank Sugg Ltd which supplied non-essential items like cricket bats and football boots. Competition in the less buoyant market was intense. Nevertheless, to outward appearances the company continued to trade successfully, including through its mail-order business, to publish substantial catalogues and to advertise in the usual places. But the company had over-reached itself. Additional branches it had opened since the war, and in particular its investments in the Netherlands, proved costly mistakes. Like many companies before and since, the Sugg brothers and their co-directors found that it was no easy matter to manage the process of expanding to a much larger scale of business, especially when the total market was not growing. The anticipated profits turned into losses, £4,972 0s 11d in the year to 31 January 1921. The company's bankers demanded the repayment of loans.

In an effort to remedy the situation, a capital reconstruction was undertaken with the Philip Mead Bat Co. Ltd, a business founded in 1919 and incorporated the following year, taking up a majority shareholding and promising additional funding.[105] Herbert Hooper and Edgar Jay of the Philip Mead Bat Company were appointed directors of Frank Sugg Ltd. By these events, Frank and Walter surrendered legal control of the company they had built up. Soon after, Frank Sugg Ltd's manufacturing operations were discontinued and the Philip Mead Bat Company became the manufacturing arm of the two companies. The head office of Frank

105 Philip Mead, the Hampshire cricketer, was a partner in a sports retail business in Southampton, but had almost no personal involvement in the bat-making business bearing his name, as can be seen in Neil Jenkinson's full account of Mead's life, *Hampshire's Greatest Run-maker*, published by Paul Cave in 1993. It is not known how the Sugg brothers made contact with this competitor business.

Sugg Ltd was transferred from Liverpool to the Philip Mead Bat Company's head office at 54 Great Eastern Street, Shoreditch, on the edge of the City of London. Walter Sugg was replaced as managing director by Edgar Jay, who sought to exercise detailed control from the centre. This caused much unrest in Sugg branches around the country. Relations between the Sugg brothers, who continued as directors, and Edgar Jay and other Philip Mead Bat Company top managers were strained from the outset and were compounded as it became clear that the financial difficulties of the Philip Mead Bat Company meant that it was unable to provide all the additional finance it had promised. For Frank Sugg Ltd matters went from bad to worse. In the year to 31 January 1922, a net loss of £29,170 12s 11d was recorded. With continuing and mounting losses came further changes in the directors and increased borrowing, including from the Philip Mead Bat Company. There were serious problems in maintaining adequate supplies of the wide range of products to the branches and quality standards slipped. Customer complaints increased.

Through 1923 the company struggled to keep afloat. Bills went unpaid and cheques bounced. Internal documents show how seriously relations between Frank Sugg and his co-directors deteriorated as the company slid towards the abyss. Frank made little effort to hide his disagreement with the way the business was being run or his hostility towards Edgar Jay.[106] He may have been a good team-player on the cricket field but that could not be said of his later years in the world of business. A major slimming-down of the Frank Sugg business might have saved it, but backbiting within the top management undermined all attempts to work towards a solution.[107] The financial difficulties proved too serious to staunch and on 18 December 1923 a winding-up order was made by the High Court upon petitions presented by the company's creditors on 3 and 4 December 1923. A Receiver was appointed to carry out the winding-up. During 1924 the process of selling branches, stock and other company assets got underway. The Frank Sugg business was effectively dead, even though it continued to trade in a minor way through the mail until the Receiver had completed his work.

106 In September 1923 Frank Sugg sued the company he had founded for monies he claimed were due to him and was then banned from entering any premises of Frank Sugg Ltd until a settlement was reached. Countering, the company chairman accused Frank of giving inadequate attention to the affairs of the business and wasting his colleagues' time 'by telling filthy yarns'.

107 In a note he scribbled on one letter, Frank Sugg referred to how 'they smoothed us over with lying promises.' He also claimed minutes of meetings had been altered after the event.

As Frank Sugg Ltd struggled to survive, the Philip Mead Bat Company was overwhelmed by its own financial difficulties and the company was wound up in April 1924, after only five years of trading. Even the association of as celebrated a name as Philip Mead was no guarantee of commercial success in the challenging trading conditions of the 1920s.

During the period when Frank Sugg Ltd was being wound up, a strange full-page advertisement appeared in the 1926 issue of *Wisden*. It was headed 'Lt & Qmr Frank Sugg' who was described as the 'Return Mail Order Man", and it declared: 'There is only one Frank Sugg in the Athletic Trade and his only address is 10 North John Street, Liverpool. No connection with any other firm.' Frank Sugg is described as 'Lancashire County and All England Eleven and Captain of Everton, Burnley, Sheffield, Derby County, Bolton Football Clubs.' It carries Frank Sugg's signature but there are number of oddities about it. The reference to Sheffield rather than Sheffield Wednesday, and the erroneous claim that Frank Sugg was captain of all the football clubs named is one of them. Then there are the military titles. *The London Gazette* of 13 May 1919 records that F.H.Sugg had relinquished his commission after his period of service with the military while retaining the rank of lieutenant, but the obvious question is why Frank, a well-known sportsman, should want to advertise himself in *Wisden* in 1926 in such a way, several years after the end of hostilities. The address, 10 North John Street, is featured as 'his only address'. It looks as if Frank was seeking to distance himself from the failed Frank Sugg Ltd and Philip Mead Bat Company Ltd businesses – 'no connection with any other firm' – and to make an attempt to continue on his own account – 'the return mail order man'. I have seen no follow-ups to the 1926 advertisement but Liverpool directories after 1927 refer to 'Frank Sugg (himself) Athletic Outfitter', suggesting that Frank did continue some kind of business from his own home, by this time at 65 St Johns Road. But the truth is that no effective new Frank Sugg business emerged from the wreckage of Frank Sugg Ltd. The company was finally formally dissolved on 16 June 1931.

Despite the growing difficulties of his business – or perhaps because of them – Frank had a keen eye for any other business opportunities. After the war he entered into some highly speculative ventures, for example for the sale of surplus war goods. Some of these also failed. According to his granddaughter, Lorna Brown, Frank 'went bust' on more than one occasion. She recalled being told of the bailiffs arriving at the family home and Frank's daughters secreting in their clothing some of his more valuable glassware. The collapse of his sports business did not mean that Frank Sugg personally was bankrupt - the fate which befell his rival, Edgar Jay, when the Philip Mead Bat Company went under - but he did lose his remaining investment in the company and any prospect of future income from that source.

It is worth adding a short comment on the fortunes of HHB Sugg Ltd, a separate business, though many people have assumed that it was the original business founded by Frank and Walter in 1888 in a different corporate guise. After the initial purchase of shops from Frank Sugg Ltd, the Sheffield-based firm expanded and opened additional branches in the area. Ultimately HHB Sugg Ltd had 11 branches, making it a larger business, in branch numbers, than Frank Sugg Ltd ever was. It was, indeed, one of the largest sports goods companies in the country. The Second World War brought disaster. The Snig Hill branch, and another at Angel Street in Sheffield, were bombed in the Sheffield blitz of December 1941. New premises were found after the war in Pinstone Street, which became the headquarters and flagship store of the company, and Castle Street. As the economy recovered and a consumer boom followed the austerity years, the business prospered. It diversified from sports equipment and clothing into toys, electrical and other household appliances. HHB Sugg Ltd became one of the leading retail businesses in Sheffield, even being described as a Sheffield icon in one newspaper report.

One unfortunate consequence of the bombing of HHB Sugg Ltd premises was that documents relating to the early days of the two Sugg businesses were destroyed. This has added to the difficulty of establishing the trading relationship between the two businesses. There must have been problems over the use of the Sugg brand name, especially on Sugg cricket bats. The bats sold by HHB Sugg Ltd in the early years would have included bats produced by Frank Sugg Ltd and carrying Frank's name and later Philip Mead bats, but in the 1930s HHB Sugg Ltd set up its own bat-making business in Sheffield, The Sugg Manufacturing Co Ltd with its own stand of willow trees - in the then proprietor's garden. HHB Sugg's bats were branded Sugg Exelsa and its premium bats were endorsed and signed by well-known cricketers, for example, the Willie Watson Autograph bat. But the aim of the business was to meet the needs of players of all ages and standards. Although

The Sugg Manufacturing Company Ltd made other products than cricket bats – the company proudly boasted that its footballs were used in the FA Cup Final for many years – all of which were branded Sugg Exelsa, cricket bats and equipment were the sports goods most associated with the Sugg name. As the company's reputation grew, it sold willow to other bat manufacturers: the Stuart Surridge bat-making business was one of its best customers. However, faced by increasing competition from Far Eastern bat manufacturers in particular, Sugg Manufacturing folded in the late 1970s, and home-produced bats and other equipment were replaced mainly by imported products.

Whether by agreement or not, HHB Sugg Ltd did not engage in advertising in the cricket periodicals in the years when Frank Sugg Ltd was still in active business. During the 1920s, however, the position had changed and the firm began to advertise in a range of cricket publications. Pre-war advertisements for HHB Sugg Ltd products frequently carried the slogan 'The World Famous Sports Outfitter', a phrase which served to lead most people to assume that the HHB Sugg business was a continuation of the earlier Frank Sugg business rather than a quite separate entity. Reflecting its wide product range, which after the Second World War included well-known brands of toys such as Hornby and Meccano, the firm advertised extensively in magazines and in the local newspapers.

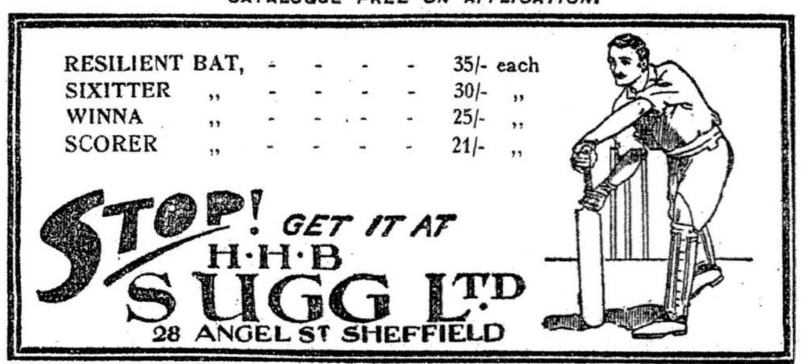

LEATHER CRICKET BALLS, 6/6, 8/6, 10/6, 12/6.
(All Warranted)
" " " Youths, 5/6, 8/6.
Leg Guards, 6/6. Batting Gloves, 6/6. Wickets, 7/6, 10/6, 12/6.

A 1922 advertisement of the HHB Sugg business that had split off from Frank Sugg Ltd in 1913.

Walter Sugg's son Bert continued to be involved in HHB Sugg Ltd until after his ninetieth birthday, but effective direction of the company passed first to his son Hubert Henri Michael Sugg, a solicitor with no great interest in cricket, and then to his grandson Hubert Henri Timothy Sugg, who has a passionate interest in the game and who had the task of managing the business in increasingly difficult times.

The development of new leisure activities for more affluent and sophisticated consumers, the growth of fashion sports and leisurewear, and the incursion into the market of large multiple retailers with greater buying power and other advantages created trading difficulties for a traditional business like HHB Sugg Ltd. It found it difficult to adapt to the changes. As the company's losses mounted, in December 2000 it announced that the business would close unless a new owner could be found. A possible merger with GT Sports came to nothing and most of the business was then sold to a local businessman who, after failing to revive its fortunes, sold it on to Streetwise Sports of Lancashire. Then, with mounting debts, this company put HHB Sugg Ltd into liquidation in March 2001.

So ended 113 years of history that had begun with the establishment of the original Sugg business in Liverpool by Frank and Walter Sugg.

Chapter Eleven
Umpire and Journalist

Perhaps seeking to fill the void in his life after the decline of his business, Frank persuaded the Lancashire committee in 1925 to nominate him as an umpire for first-class matches. Counties liked to help their former players where they could and Frank's name was put forward despite his age and the length of time he had been away from first-class cricket.[108] There was no training course or assessment process. It was up to the committee of county captains to make the final selection. 'Tiger' Smith described his own selection: 'The powers that be assumed I knew the Laws and all I had to do was turn up in my white coat at the start of the 1921 season.'[109] It was the same for Frank Sugg and his name was duly included in the list of 24 umpires for the 1926 season. He remained on the list for the following season.

Frank Sugg stood in 46 first-class matches in 1926 and 1927, mainly County Championship fixtures but including two matches of the visiting Australians in 1926 and two of the visiting New Zealanders in 1927. None of the county matches involved Lancashire, Derbyshire or Yorkshire. His first match was Nottinghamshire's game against Northamptonshire at Trent Bridge starting on 1 May 1926 and his last was Warwickshire against Surrey at Edgbaston, commencing 17 August 1927. He enjoyed umpiring and seems to have carried out his duties competently enough.[110]

Frank considered himself well qualified to be a first-class umpire: he had experience of the game at the highest level, he was a

108 At the time Frank, then aged 64, was the oldest practitioner who had been taken on to the English first-class umpires list. Only Percy Mills, the former Gloucestershire player, has since been older: he joined the list a few days before his 68th birthday, at the start of the 1947 season. Like Sugg he was listed for just a couple of seasons. My thanks to Philip Bailey for his help on this point.

109 *Tiger Smith*, as told to Pat Murphy, Lutterworth Press, 1981, p 74.

110 Sir Home Gordon, admittedly not always a reliable witness, commented in *Background of Cricket*, published by Arthur Barker in 1939, p 146, that, as an umpire, Sugg scandalised 'the old school' by 'being invariably bareheaded, setting a fashion since widely emulated.'

student of the Laws of the game, he had good eyesight and hearing, even at his relatively advanced age, and, he would claim, a common-sense approach to the job. If he had a weakness it was perhaps suspect powers of concentration which had certainly been his undoing as a player in many instances. Frank had a rapport with the players that came with many years of playing the game at the top level. He was never reluctant to offer an explanation for his decisions and could be quick to remind a player who was in charge. When a county captain objected to a couple of his decisions, Frank offered him his white coat with the words: 'If you think you can do better, you should put this on.'

Frank was very critical of the way umpires were selected and of their pay and conditions.[111] He thought it outrageous that it should be county captains rather than some independent body who decided who should be added to the umpires' list. He also objected to the system where umpires were graded, in secret, as good, indifferent or bad by county captains and could be struck off the list if they collected three bad grades in the course of a season with no right of appeal. In contrast, if an umpire wanted to report a player for ungentlemanly conduct he must first inform the player's captain when, odds on, the player would offer an apology to end the matter.

At Frank Sugg's time, an umpire was paid £9 10s 0d for a match starting on a Wednesday, £10 10s 0d for a match starting on a Saturday. From this fee, the umpire had to meet his travel and hotel expenses. Given the irregularity of the employment, Frank Sugg reckoned he would be lucky to make £100 in a season. And he found the job tiring. He argued that an improvement in umpires' pay and conditions was essential if umpires of an acceptable quality were to be attracted and retained. If Frank made his views known at the highest level of the game - and it would certainly be characteristic of him to have done so - it had little effect. Umpires continued to be poorly paid. Whether by his own choice or otherwise, Frank was not re-appointed as an umpire for the 1928 season. He was one of four who were stood down. Among the replacements was William Phillips, already an experienced umpire (he stood in two Test matches in 1921), who had played a few games for Lancashire in the first decade of the century.

---

111 His comments will be found in his column in *Liverpool Echo*, 18 May 1929.

As another way of earning some money by making use of his knowledge of the game, Frank turned to journalism. In earlier times a number of sportsmen were paid by newspapers or periodicals to write on their sports, notable examples in cricket being Ranjitsinhji, C.B.Fry and P.F.Warner. Following their lead, Frank was engaged by the *Liverpool Echo* for a number of years to write a weekly article on cricket during the season for the paper's Saturday edition. 'Frank Sugg, the old Lancashire cricketer, gives our readers the benefit of his ripe experience in dealing with problems on the field,' trumpeted the *Echo*. It is not known how much Frank was paid for his articles. His column was syndicated to other papers in the Liverpool area such as *Buff*, the Saturday sports edition of the *Bolton Evening News*, and therefore had a wide circulation. The articles in the *Echo* were of several column inches in length and were invariably of a serious nature. Frank had no time for gossip and sensationalism (in so far as this was permissible in the media at the time). There is little doubt that the articles were Frank's own work. After all, he had written for his *Pocket Cricket Annual* for a number of years. One feels that Frank Sugg would have had no truck with the idea of a ghost writer though no doubt he was helped by his colleagues on the paper. One of these expressed admiration for his work on the occasion of Frank's death.

The serious flavour of Frank's journalism can be gathered by mention of a few of the articles published in May and June 1929. The 11 May article was headed 'Flaws in the Management of County Cricket' and called for the establishment of a County Cricket Association to take over the functions exercised by MCC and its Advisory Committee. He regarded MCC as too elitist an organisation 'to take upon itself a complete domination of county clubs'. He believed the proposed change would correct the discrimination that he perceived against players from the North and Midlands in the selection of Test teams. Frank was writing ahead of his time, as he was in articles that urged action to remove 'shamateurism' from the game. The article of 18 May, headed 'The Airy Pedestal of the County Umpire', argued for an improvement in the pay and conditions of umpires and in the way they were appointed and called for 'an exhaustive enquiry' into all aspects of the umpire's role and position. On 1 June in an article headed 'Ruling Pad Play out of Cricket', Frank deplored the growing use of pad play and the readiness of batsmen to dispute leg-before decisions by claiming they had touched the ball before the pad was struck. On 22 June, under the headline 'Grass for the Lads', he urged his readers to support campaigns to provide cricket facilities for elementary schools. Speaking from his own experience, he said many youngsters with an aptitude for cricket were lost to the game simply because they had nowhere to play but the back streets.

The articles attracted quite a postbag and Frank was assiduous in responding to his readers' comments and queries in subsequent articles. He seems to have been particularly keen to engage in discussion about the Laws of the game. For example, in one article, on 15 June, he debated at length a reader's suggestion that it should be irrelevant where a ball pitched in making leg-before-wicket decisions. Frank accepted that such a change would simplify the umpire's task but he concluded it would be a retrograde step because it would considerably shorten games and be financially harmful.

A favourite of spectators for his bravado performances at the crease, Frank Sugg's journalism reveals how deeply he thought about the game and how it needed to be changed, in his view, to make it even better and more enjoyable.

Chapter Twelve
A Sad End

As he approached his seventieth birthday, for the first time Frank found himself with time on his hands. His business had closed and his foray into journalism had ended. But Frank Sugg was not a man to take to his armchair with his favourite pipe in his home at 65 St Johns Road in Waterloo. He helped in the running of another sports business in the area - probably that of his sometime Lancashire colleague Jack Sharp - and he maintained his keen interest in the fortunes of the local sports clubs with which he had been associated. Acquaintances he encountered on his walks or journeys at this time commented how well he looked and how ready he was to relive his own exploits with the cricket bat or billiard cue. But underneath the surface all was not so rosy.

65 St Johns Road, Waterloo - Dorlins shop - in 2011.
This is where Frank Sugg lived in his later years until his death in 1933; the shop conversion has taken place since his time.

The worry and acrimony that accompanied the last years of the Sugg business had taken their toll. During those years, Walter Sugg had been the rock on which his more tempestuous brother could lean. Walter and Frank were near neighbours and their relationship had always been close. Now Frank could no longer rely on Walter for support. With the collapse of the business, Walter moved back to Derbyshire, more precisely to Dore, then a village on the outskirts of Sheffield and soon to be incorporated into the city and therefore into Yorkshire. This enabled him to be closer to his own family and the son who was running HHB Sugg Ltd, as we have seen a separate business to Frank Sugg Ltd. For a while Walter had an advisory role with the company.

Walter suffered poor health after his move to Dore. Indeed, he spent much of his final years confined to his bed. He died on 21 May 1933, his 73rd birthday. He was buried two days later in the family plot in Burngreave Cemetery in Sheffield after a funeral attended by family members, local dignitaries and representatives of local cricket clubs and organisations. A two-minutes silence was held before all matches in the Sugg Thursday League on 25 May 1933 as a mark of respect.

Walter's death was a great shock to Frank and hit him badly. But he did not attend Walter's funeral. Frank was not in as good health as his acquaintances in Liverpool had supposed and he must have felt unable to face the journey to Sheffield and the emotion of the day.[112] Indeed, Frank died suddenly at his home on 29 May 1933, from heart failure, just eight days after his brother's death and six days after Walter's funeral.[113] He was 71 years old.

As with Walter, Frank's funeral was quickly arranged. It took place at St Luke's church in Crosby, a couple of miles from his home at Waterloo, on 1 June 1933. Dating from 1853 and in the Gothic style characteristic of the time, St Luke's seems a fitting place for the funeral of a leading cricketer of the late Victorian years. Among the mourners at the funeral were Frank's son, Frank Reginald, his three daughters with their respective spouses (Mr and Mrs W.Morgan, Mr and Mrs Richard R.Tippin, and Mr and Mrs W.Neville), a sister (Mrs W.Chadwick), Walter's son, Bert, and Bert's

112 A writer in *The Cricketer* referred to a conversation some three weeks before his death in a Liverpool to Southport train about Frank's innings of 171 for Lancashire against Oxford University in 1890 when 'he looked quite well'.

113 The death certificate gives the cause of death as 'Aortic Incompetence'. Today a more precise cause of death would be expected.

son, Hubert Henri Michael. In Bert's case, duty and propriety prevailed over any ill-feelings he had had towards Frank. But Frank's widow did not attend. *The Waterloo and Crosby Herald* of 3 June 1933 carried a brief account of the funeral; it reported that 'many others' attended the funeral and 'many beautiful floral tributes were sent by relatives and friends.'

According to the church's records, Frank was buried at St Luke's.[114] Yet there is no headstone to mark Frank Sugg's final resting place. Indeed, he is buried in a public and unmarked grave, often the fate of paupers. This fact was first reported by Philip Paine with the comment: 'A sad end for such a talented man.'[115] A sad end indeed: not only does the grave have no headstone, its exact location has been lost. The part of St Luke's graveyard that contains the public graves is overgrown with long grass, brambles and elderberry bushes, with just the occasional stone tablet marking the ground's purpose.

Neither Lorna Brown, his granddaughter, nor Timothy Sugg, his brother's great-grandson, were aware of the place and nature of Frank Sugg's grave and they could offer no explanation of why the grave should have been left unmarked. Timothy Sugg had always assumed that Frank had been buried in the family plot in Burngreave Cemetery, Sheffield. For certainty, I checked the cemetery records and they confirm that Frank Sugg is not buried there. Lorna Brown wondered if he had been cremated. Frank apparently introduced his family to Christian Science - he was attracted by its advocacy of a healthy and positive lifestyle - and Lorna's mother and aunt became keen followers. Denying the existence of matter, including of the human body, and believing that disease and death

St Luke's Church, Crosby in 2010. Frank Sugg's funeral was conducted here in June 1933.

114 The graveyard, now virtually full, covers an area of four and a half acres.
115 Philip Paine, *Innings Complete, Volume 8*, 2004, p 45.

are only illusions, Christian Scientists prefer cremation to burial as the means of disposing of the body. Could Frank Sugg have been cremated after the funeral at St Luke's? A check of the records of crematoriums in the Liverpool drew a blank, providing no support for this possibility. However uncomfortable to family members, or surprising to anyone who has read of Frank Sugg, 'a talented man', the fact is that Frank is buried in an unmarked, public grave on the edge of St Luke's churchyard in an area also occupied by numbers of Liverpool's paupers.

What were Frank Sugg's financial circumstances at the time of his death? It is hard to say. For a start he left no will and his surviving family members have no information on the point. According to his granddaughter, the Suggs lived 'the life of Riley' in their heyday. Then Frank lost money as his sports business foundered after the First World War and also with the failure of a number of more speculative business ventures. If the suspicions of Walter Sugg's side of the family are accepted, Frank's estate might have been encumbered with accumulated gambling debts. It may be hard to believe that Frank was penniless when he died, but the possibility is that he had little or no money by that time. Even if that is the case, however, it hardly explains the absence of a headstone.[116]

His son and daughters, one or more of whom (or their spouses) might then have paid for the funeral, could have been expected to pay also for a grave and headstone at St Luke's. They were very fond of their father, they 'revered' him according to his granddaughter, and it is hard to think of a reason why they should not have wanted to erect a headstone to his memory. Bert Sugg, who had so recently buried his own father, Walter, was a wealthy man and one who would have been very aware of the proprieties of a family bereavement. Could his antipathy to Frank have been such that he was not prepared to contribute to a headstone on Frank's grave? This may seem unlikely but family feuding can have unlikely consequences. I have to admit that the reason for Frank Sugg's 'sad end' remains an intriguing mystery.[117]

116 The church authorities say they have no knowledge of Frank's circumstances at the time of his death or of why his grave has no headstone.

117 None of the many obituaries and tributes that were published after Frank Sugg's death made any reference to financial difficulties or strained relations within the Sugg family. That of course is as would be expected.

After Frank's death, his widow went to stay with her daughter Margot, who lived in Pontefract. It appears that the Lancashire County Cricket Club were made aware of the straightened circumstances in which Amy found herself. The minutes of a committee meeting on 8 June 1933, just one week after the funeral, reads as follows: 'A letter was read from Mr A.J.Barley re the affairs of the late Frank Sugg. The matter was left to Mr Stoddart, Mr Kinnear and the Secretary with power to award not exceeding £20 if necessary.' But Amy died from cardiac failure, only two months after Frank's death, while still in Pontefract. (Ill-health may have been the reason she did not attend Frank's funeral.) On news of her death, the committee, at a meeting on 10 August 1933, resolved to rescind the offered grant.[118] There were also reports that a benefit match to raise money for Frank's widow was to be arranged, probably at New Brighton, but if there were any such thoughts they were also abandoned after Amy's own death.[119]

However sad the end of Frank Sugg's life, and however puzzling the fact that he lies in an unmarked public grave, the story of his life is the story of a man who lived life to the full and brought pleasure to untold thousands with the vigour and enjoyment he brought to cricket and to the other sports at which he excelled. Nothing can detract from that.

It is thought that Frank Sugg was buried in a public grave at the foot of this section of the wall on the south-east side of St Luke's graveyard in Crosby.

118 I am grateful to Malcolm Lorimer for searching the committee minutes for this information.

119 *The Cricketer*, 6 September 1933.

Acknowledgements

I am most grateful to Lorna Brown, Frank Sugg's granddaughter, for information she has been able to provide about Frank and for sight of a scrapbook kept by Frank, mainly of newspaper photographs and cuttings (not relating just to himself). I am also grateful to Timothy Sugg, Walter Sugg's great-grandson, and to his sister Sally Ann Barrass and cousin Andrew Rodker, for recollections of Frank Sugg from their side of the family, and to Timothy for documents relating to the final years of Frank Sugg's sports business. Lorna and Timothy both read drafts of my manuscript and are content with the way I have treated those details of Frank Sugg's life about which there has to be continuing uncertainty. But any errors or misinterpretations are entirely my responsibility.

I am grateful to Malcolm Lorimer for copies of newspaper cuttings about Frank Sugg and to the late Don Ambrose for the loan of copies of Frank Sugg's *Pocket Cricket Annual*. A number of persons have provided information about Frank's activities in sports other than cricket and I have acknowledged their contributions in footnotes to the text. Lorna Brown, Andrew Rodker, Margaret Doyle of Clongowes Wood College, Ireland, have contributed illustrations, as has Roger Mann from his private collection. I thank them all.

For various reasons, this book has been a long time in the writing. I am most grateful to my editor, David Jeater, for his encouragement, patience and efficiency. I have benefited considerably from David's knowledge of cricket history and the cricket literature. I am also grateful to David Pracy for his comments on an early draft; to Brian Rendell for preparing the index; to Ray Greenall and John Ward the proofreaders; and to Peter Griffiths for his diligent typesetting and for his management of the book's production.

Above all, though, my thanks go to my wife, Anne, for her support in a project that became something of a long-running obsession.

M.H.

Bibliography

I have provided full citations of my sources in the footnotes in the book and have not listed all of them in this bibliography.

Published cricket histories and biographies give little space to Frank Sugg. Among the publications which I have found useful are:

H.S.Altham and E.W Swanton, *A History of Cricket* (Third Edition), George Allen and Unwin, 1947

Brian Bearshaw, *From the Stretford End: the Official History of Lancashire County Cricket Club*, Partridge Press, 1990

Derek Birley, *A Social History of English Cricket*, Aurum Press, 1999

Robert Brooke, *A History of the County Cricket Championship*, Guinness Publishing, 1991

Robert Brooke and David Goodyear, *Who's Who of Lancashire County Cricket Club*, Breedon Books, 1991

Michael Down, *Archie: a Biography of A.C.MacLaren*, George Allen and Unwin, 1981

W.G.Grace, *Cricket Reminiscences and Personal Recollections*, James Bowden, 1899

Rev R.S.Holmes, *The History of Yorkshire County Cricket, 1833–1903*, Archibald Constable and Co, 1904

A.W.Ledbrooke, *Lancashire County Cricket: the Official History of the Lancashire County and Manchester Cricket Club, 1864–1953*, Phoenix House, 1954

Malcolm Lorimer, *Lancashire Cricketers: 1865–1988*, ACS Publications, 1989

Eric Midwinter, *Red Roses Crest the Caps: the Story of Lancashire County Cricket Club*, The Kingswood Press, 1989

Pat Murphy, *Tiger Smith*, Lutterworth Press, 1981

Philip Paine, *Innings Complete, Volume 8*, Mischief Makers, 2004

F.G.Peach, *Derbyshire Cricketers: 1871–1981*, ACS Publications, 1981

Anthony Woodhouse, *Who's Who of Yorkshire County Cricket Club*, Breedon Books, 1992

Ric Sissons, *The Players: A Social History of the Professional Cricketer*, The Kingswood Press, 1988

Joseph Stoddart, *Men I Have Met*, J.Heywood, 1889

Jack Williams, *Cricket in England*, Taylor and Francis, 2003

Peter Wynne-Thomas, *The History of Lancashire County Cricket Club*, Christopher Helm, 1989

My main sources in writing this book have been newspapers, national and local, and cricket periodicals. As mentioned in the acknowledgements section, I have benefited from collections of Press cuttings made available to me by Malcolm Lorimer and Lorna Brown. The following contain particularly useful profiles of Frank Sugg: *Cricket* magazines of 12 July 1888 and 23 April 1896 and the *Sporting Chronicle* of 25 July, 1916. *Cricket* magazine of 28 May 1896 includes a profile of Walter Sugg.

Invaluable sources have, of course, been *Wisden Cricketers' Almanacks* and the scorecard and biographical information at cricketarchive.com.

Appendix

Career Statistics

Test Cricket: Batting and Fielding

	M	*I*	*NO*	*R*	*HS*	*Ave*	*100*	*50*	*Ct*
1888	2	2	0	55	31	27.50	-	-	-

Notes: Both Sugg's matches were against Australia; he did not bowl in either match.

First-Class Cricket: Batting and Fielding

	M	*I*	*NO*	*R*	*HS*	*Ave*	*100*	*50*	*Ct/St*
1883	8	12	4	80	13*	10.00	-	-	4/1
1884	13	26	0	439	73	16.88	-	3	11
1885	10	19	2	462	187	27.17	1	1	6
1886	12	23	0	408	62	17.73	-	1	3
1887	8	15	1	417	98	29.78	-	3	7
1888	19	31	2	565	102*	19.48	1	1	10
1889	20	30	2	747	89	26.67	-	4	12
1890	23	39	2	796	171	21.51	1	3	10
1891	18	27	1	557	75	21.42	-	2	7
1892	19	30	1	705	107*	24.31	1	3	15
1893	24	44	2	1047	169*	24.92	3	4	13
1894	24	42	4	1033	157*	27.18	2	5	14
1895	23	38	1	847	125	22.89	1	2	13
1896	29	49	3	1439	220	31.28	3	4	14
1897	26	37	3	1023	122	30.08	1	8	16
1898	23	42	1	1044	169	25.46	2	5	9
1899	6	11	1	250	95	25.00	-	1	3
Career	**305**	**515**	**30**	**11859**	**220**	**24.45**	**16**	**50**	**167/1**

Notes: Sugg was dismissed 236 times caught (49%); 195 times bowled (40%); 20 times lbw (4%); 18 times run out (4%) and 16 times stumped (3%). He was dismissed most often by J.T.Hearne, 18 times; G.A.Lohmann, 17 times; and by W.Attewell, 16 times. He played in 234 matches for Lancashire, scoring 9,648 runs at 25.37 including 15 centuries, and taking 130 catches.

First-Class Cricket: Bowling

	O	*M*	*R*	*W*	*BB*	*Ave*	*5i*
1885	6	1	14	0	-	-	-
1887	16	1	49	2	2-20	24.50	-
1888	3	0	9	0	-	-	-

1894		13	2	45	2	2-34	22.50	-
1895		4	0	16	0	-	-	-
1896		24	2	77	4	2-29	19.25	-
1897		6	0	25	0	-	-	-
1898		11.2	1	35	2	2-12	17.50	-
1899		1	0	3	0	-	-	-
Career	**(4b)**	**25**	**2**					
	(5b)	**59.2**	**5**	**273**	**10**	**2-12**	**27.30**	**-**

Notes: Overs were of four balls in 1885, 1887 and 1888 and of five balls from 1894 to 1899. Sugg took wickets at the rate of one per 39.70 balls and conceded runs at a rate equivalent to 4.12 runs per six-ball over. Six of his ten wickets were caught, three bowled and one stumped.

First-Class Cricket: Centuries (16)

Score	For	Opponent	Venue	Season
187	Derbyshire[1]	Hampshire	Southampton	1885
102*	Lancashire[1]	Gloucestershire	Gloucester (Spa)	1888
171	Lancashire[1]	Oxford University	Old Trafford	1890
107*	Lancashire[1]	Surrey	Old Trafford	1892
169*	Lancashire[1]	Sussex	Old Trafford	1893
127	Lancashire[1]	Nottinghamshire	Trent Bridge	1893
127	Lancashire[1]	Gloucestershire	Old Trafford	1893
105	Lancashire[1]	Somerset	Old Trafford	1894
157*	Lancashire[1]	Somerset	Taunton	1894
125	Lancashire[2]	Kent	Tonbridge	1895
110	Lancashire[1]	Sussex	Old Trafford	1896
220	Lancashire[1]	Gloucestershire	Bristol	1896
151	Lancashire[1]	Leicestershire	Leicester (GR)	1896
122	Lancashire[1]	Yorkshire	Old Trafford	1897
169	Lancashire[2]	Somerset	Taunton	1898
104	Lancashire[1]	Essex	Old Trafford	1898

Notes: The index figures [1] and [2] above indicate the innings in which the century was scored.

Umpiring

Frank Sugg was on the first-class umpires list for two seasons, 1926 and 1927, standing in 46 first-class matches.

Walter Sugg

Walter, Frank's older brother, played one first-class match for Yorkshire in 1881 and 128 matches for Derbyshire from 1884 to 1887 and from 1894 to 1902. In 129 first-class matches, he scored 3,469 runs at 17.17, including two centuries, took 50 wickets at 31.20, and held 64 catches.

Sources: cricketarchive.com and Wisden Cricketers' Almanacks.

Index

A page number in bold type indicates an illustration.